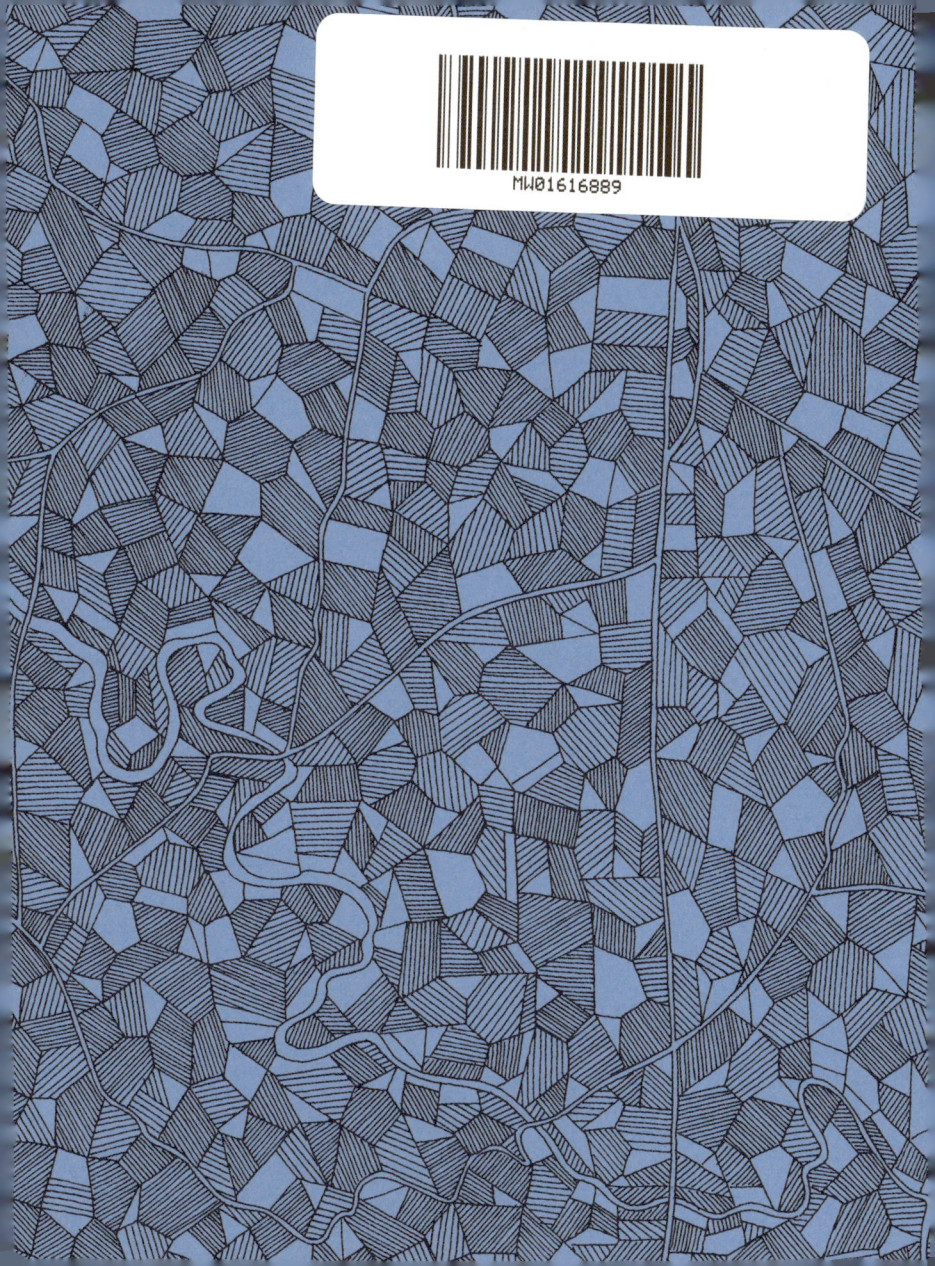

Conversations
on the Coast

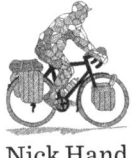

Nick Hand

Published by The Department of Small Works

First published in 2011 by The Department
of Small Works, Bristol, England.

Photography © 2011 Nick Hand

Transcripts have been edited from
original recordings and printed with
kind permission of their authors.

A CIP catalogue record for this book is
available from the British Library.

ISBN 978-0-9569332-0-1

Edited and designed by The Department
of Small Works with special thanks to
Rachel Miller.

Illustrations by Millie Marotta.

Printed on Naturalis and Colorplan by
GF Smith. Both papers are manufactured
in the UK and accredited by the Forest
Stewardship Council.

Printed and bound in Wales at
Gomer Press, Llandysul, Ceredigion.

For Walter Horace Hand,
cyclist, carpenter and gentleman.

Foreword

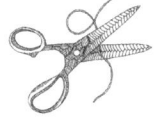

It has never been a better time to put emphasis back on the importance of craftsmanship in a world which is full of too much product and too much of everything. Individuality and true craftsmanship is something that we really need. Also a change of attitude, especially with the younger generation, to be more humble in their approach to life and not only be motivated by power and money.

Being satisfied with the skill that you have in your hands, pacing yourself to learn a craft, and developing it, is such an important thing for the future.

Paul Smith

Acknowledgements

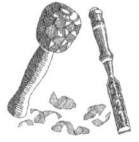

This book is dedicated to everyone that gave up their time to talk about their work, their lives and their passion: Brian Alabaster, Fraser Anderson, Kay Anderson, Kenny Anderson, Mr Aylesbury, Jeremy Barker, Marcus Beck, Mervyn Bennallack, Bill Bontoft, Ronnie Bowie, Nicola Bradley, Billy Bragg, Austin Brown, Will Brown, Hilary Burns, Cally, Martin Carter, Chris and Neil Cobbett, Jackson Conn, David Cooper, Mikey Corker, Mark Cousins, Merlin Crossingham, Darren Cunningham, Harold Cunningham, Angela and Carl Daly, Sheena Devitt, Stephanie Diver, Avalon dos Santos, Martin Doyle, Hugh Dunford Wood, Ailbhe Dunne, Laurence Edwards, Gunhild Espelage, Neil and Gill Faiers, Tom Ferguson, Aideen Fitzpatrick, Claire Francis, Martina Gavan, Joanna and Donald Gisbey, Lotte Glob, Sarah Green, Douglas Grierson, Christiane Guenther, Dawn and Erin Hackutt, John Halls, John Joseph Hanna, Keith Hannah, Keith Harrison, Karl Harron, Billy Hawkins, Karen Hay-Edie, Suki Hays-Watkins, David Hewitt, Clare Hieatt, John Hogan, Jenna Hume, Louis Hunkin, Joanne B Kaar, Fiona Kelly, Paul F Kelly, Graham King, Nigel Legge, Dominique Lieb, Sam Lindo, Clive Lyttle, Mary MacAlister Hall, John MacPherson, Simon Macro, James MacTaggart, Darren Matthews, Ruth McCartney, Alan McDougall, Midge McKeachie, John McKenna, Jo McLean, Mike Mial, Jackie Miller, Joanne Mitchell, Allan Moller, Beth Moran, Helen Moriarty, David Morris, Chris Morton, Zoe Murphy, Howie R Nicholsby, Rory O'Connell, Pádraig Ó Duinnín, Brian O'Grady, Fearghal O'Nuallain, Louise Oppenheimer, Merle Osbourne, Matt Padwick, John Parry, Julian Pearce, Elsie Pinniger, Emrys Plant, Quay Proctor-Mears, Keira Rathbone, Rosalind Redfern, Graham Roberts, Mark Roberts, John J Savage, Nicole Schumacher, Peter Segger, Diane Shaw, Chiara Shokite,

Paul Smith, Bill Spink, Tilda Swinton, Pat Tanner, Sue Jane Taylor, Paul Topham, Luke Van Doorslaer, Alan Walker, Pip Weaser, John Wilkinson, Bea Williams and James Yorkston. Thanks also to: Paul from Chesterfield; Ruth and Annette from Southsea; Hans from Germany; visitors to Antony Gormley's *Another Place*; and visitors to the Eric Morecambe memorial.

I also want to dedicate the book to the folk I met on the road. I suppose in our day-to-day lives we meet so many people almost in a businessy kind of way, but on the road you become much closer to your emotions and the people you meet —even for just a short period— become great friends. It's hard to explain, but it changes you and you carry this with you for a long time afterwards. Thanks to the amazing people who rode with me, fed me, gave me a bed, stayed up late and nattered: old friends and new friends. I want to give a special mention to Mike Carter, who was cycling around the coast at the same time (but in the opposite direction), and also to Jeremy Haywood —who did the same trip in the eighties— for his enthusiasm and encouragement.

From the very first, there were a group of people who encouraged me and generally made the whole idea become real. I want to thank my wife Harriet for supporting me and helping out all along the way. Thanks also to: my good friends David and Clare Hieatt running the Do Lectures in Wales, who encouraged me on this adventure; the legendary Tim March for his coaching throughout the ride; my friends at Howies in Cardigan and Bristol for their continuous support and help throughout the trip (including a great welcome home party); Argos Racing Cycles for my beautiful bike; Simon Calder at Bikehike for building the map that allowed everyone to follow me online; Kate and

Al at Positive for the website; Dan and Melissa at South West Screen; Brooks of England for the brilliant B17 special saddle and panniers; Dan and Ceri and all the folks at Innocent for a constant supply of smoothies and spreading the word of the trip; Simon Mottram at Rapha for the cycling gear; Martin at Skins; Martin at Lyon for the Tubus racks and Gary at Oakley for replacing the glasses I left on a gate post on the Orkneys.

Last but not least, I was overwhelmed by the support of people who followed my journey. Thanks for the messages, the sponsorship, the offers of places to stay and recommendations of where to get the best cakes. It helped me keep going.

Without these people the project wouldn't have been possible. Here are some great words from a hero of mine that say more than I could.

> "I'd like to say that people can change anything they want to; and that means everything in the world. Show me any country and there'll be people in it. And it's the people that make the country... It's time to take that humanity back into the centre of the ring and follow that for a time. Think on that... Without people you're nothing."

Joe Strummer

Introduction

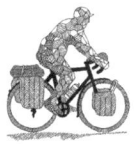

"It is by riding a bicycle that you learn the contours of a country best, since you have to sweat up the hills and coast down them. Thus you remember them as they actually are, while in a motor car only a high hill impresses you, and you have no such accurate remembrance of the country you have driven through as you gain by riding a bicycle."

Ernest Hemingway

In an idle moment, on a cycling holiday in Cornwall, I wondered how far it would be before you got back to the same point if you just carried on cycling along the coast.

The thing about an idea is that once you've told two or three people you kind of feel like you have to do it. So, a year later, I found myself setting off from my home in Bristol on a 4541-mile journey around the British coastline in a clockwise direction. Clockwise, because I liked the idea of being a little nearer the sea. That was the summer of 2009 and to complete the journey I set off again in 2010 to Ireland, to follow the coast for 1783-miles from Belfast to Belfast. I don't think I was ever fully prepared for what it would be like, but I was attracted by the simplicity of it and —as a friend said to me— there was little chance of getting lost if I kept the sea on my left and just kept going.

I've never been a serious cyclist, but I don't like cars: don't like being in them and don't like the way I feel at the end of a journey. I feel almost the complete opposite about being on a bicycle. Bicycles are friendly and sociable and I always feel better at the end of a journey.

Spending five months on a bicycle gave me all the benefits of travelling slowly. I experienced the best of our islands and the bicycle led me to some amazing people. I called the journey Slowcoast.

A few books about journeys have inspired me. One of these is Laurie Lee's *As I Walked Out One Midsummer Morning*. I really like how Lee tells the story through the people that he meets along the way. This became one of the main inspirations behind my idea of meeting artisans as I travelled and making little photofilms of them talking about their work and their life. I saw artisan as having a really broad meaning, it could be craftsmen and women but could also be a musician, an actor or a fisherman — just someone who makes their living from a specific skill and spends their time doing something they are really passionate about. It seems like a lot to achieve while I was also coping with cycling every day, but I was attracted to the challenge of seeing how much I could do on the road.

I originally set out to make about 50 films, not realising then that I would get so many great introductions and links to people I could visit. The nature of the trip meant that the day-to-day planning was minimal and I could take detours and make stops to see people. Each day I didn't know where I would end up, or which route I would take, the meetings were mostly unplanned, or quite last minute, which made them informal and relaxed. Somehow, turning up on a bicycle opens a few more doors and people seem a bit happier to have a natter.

Each meeting started with an audio recording of a conversation, and then I spent some time photographing the person, their tools and their surroundings. In the editing process, I took out my voice to just leave them telling their story and used the photographs to describe their workspace and surroundings, as well as give an insight into their personality. I got into the habit of editing the photofilms during the evening of the day I made them and uploading them to the Slowcoast website. I liked the idea that followers of the journey would be introduced to the people I was meeting almost at the same time. The photofilms had an immediacy —a bit of a rough edge— but this was all integral to the journey and the way the project developed.

In total, I made over a 100 of these little films. I called them soundslides, which is the name of the software I use to create the final film. Each one is a tribute to the people of our coastline. The accents change, but the passion people have for their work and the pride in the quality of what they create, is a constant. After talking to a few people, I noticed that there was a moment when they spoke where I felt they got to the real heart of what inspires them, where the love and the passion for what they do was strongest. That was what I set out to capture.

I reckoned the first journey would be close to 5000 miles in total. I planned to do about 50 miles a day and to do an interview about every other day. I liked the roundness of the figures — 50 miles a day, 100 days, 50 soundslides. As it happens it was a good kind of target. It allowed me to take my time and stop at any little café that took my fancy as well as fitting in visits to people's workshops and studios, leaving me with enough energy to edit and upload the films in the evening.

My friend's brother, Jeremy, did the journey in the eighties and he suggested getting a Bartholomew's Road Map and tearing out all the pages with sea on and use this as my map. Bartholomew's doesn't exist anymore —which is a shame because the Bartholomew family were keen cyclists and made sure their maps were bike friendly— but the theory was good and worked as well with an A–Z road map. These paper maps were for navigating, but I also carried a lot of technology with me. I had a little gizmo on my bike that enabled me to upload my exact route each night to the website — it showed my distance, how much I climbed each day and my exact speed. One thing I quite liked about it is that it also showed where I went wrong and where I got lost. I also relied on my phone for keeping in contact with people and to give me internet connection when I was camped out on the side of a loch in the middle of nowhere. Then I had the camera kit and the laptop. None of this left much room for the tent, clothes and a constant supply of chocolate, but it was just enough to do everything I wanted to do.

All of the kit I took, and the technical planning for the website, mapping and soundslides, was all helped enormously by generous support from friends. Through the website, my blog and Twitter I also got a huge amount of support from people following the journey who helped by writing about what I was doing and linking to the Slowcoast website. The effect of this was something I had never anticipated. I loved the process of interweb wizardry that was possible from the saddle.

Journeys are about discovery: finding out about ourselves, meeting new people and discovering new places. I feel lucky to have experienced every inch of our extraordinary coastline — we need to cherish and respect it. We need to get in our cars less and be outside more, and most importantly we need to slow down a bit more in order to look around. People tell me of exciting journeys in Europe or further afield, but for me I can't think of anywhere better to explore than our own beautiful islands. To look out from a saddle and study our funny quirky little ways and to do it under your own power with the quiet, slow pace of a bicycle is just perfect.

I never anticipated how powerful the collection of conversations I recorded would be. I was privileged to meet some amazingly talented folk who are working in traditional and new crafts, from potters, to musicians, to painters, to people who work on the land or sea. These craftspeople need to be recognised and celebrated for what they are doing. They need our support to survive, and I hope the next generation respects and values the tradition and skills that they can pass on. It has been incredibly hard to make a selection for this book, but I think the stories you're about to read show the diversity of skills, the passion and the character of the people I met.

People say that an adventure changes you, and I'm sure that's true. For me, I found it difficult to adjust back to my normal life. I would be constantly looking out of the window at passing cyclists, wondering where they were going and who they were going to meet.

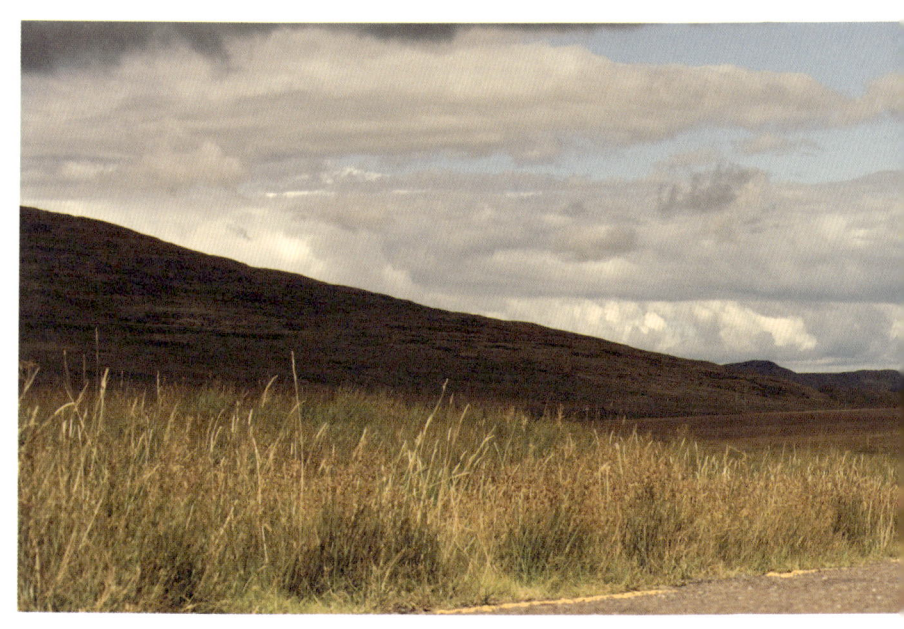

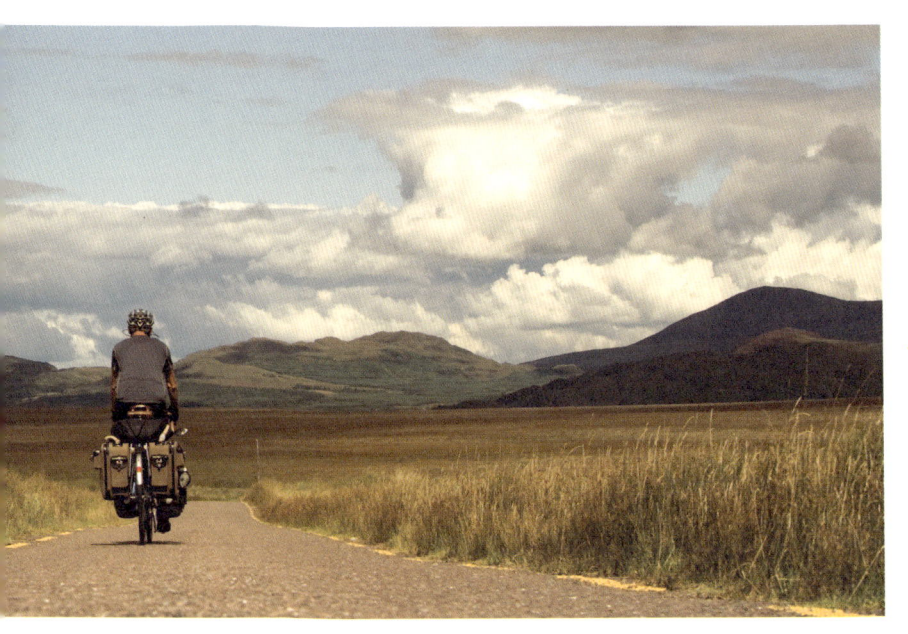

322,248 feet climbed
10,057.820 kilometres
6324.64 miles
930 hours in the saddle
137 days on the road
113 soundslides
59 blogs
6.7 mph average speed (yes, quite slow)
4 tyres
3 inner tubes
1 freewheel
1 rebuilt back wheel

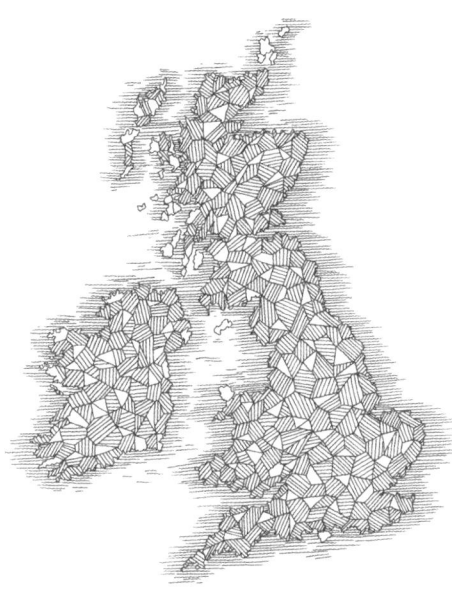

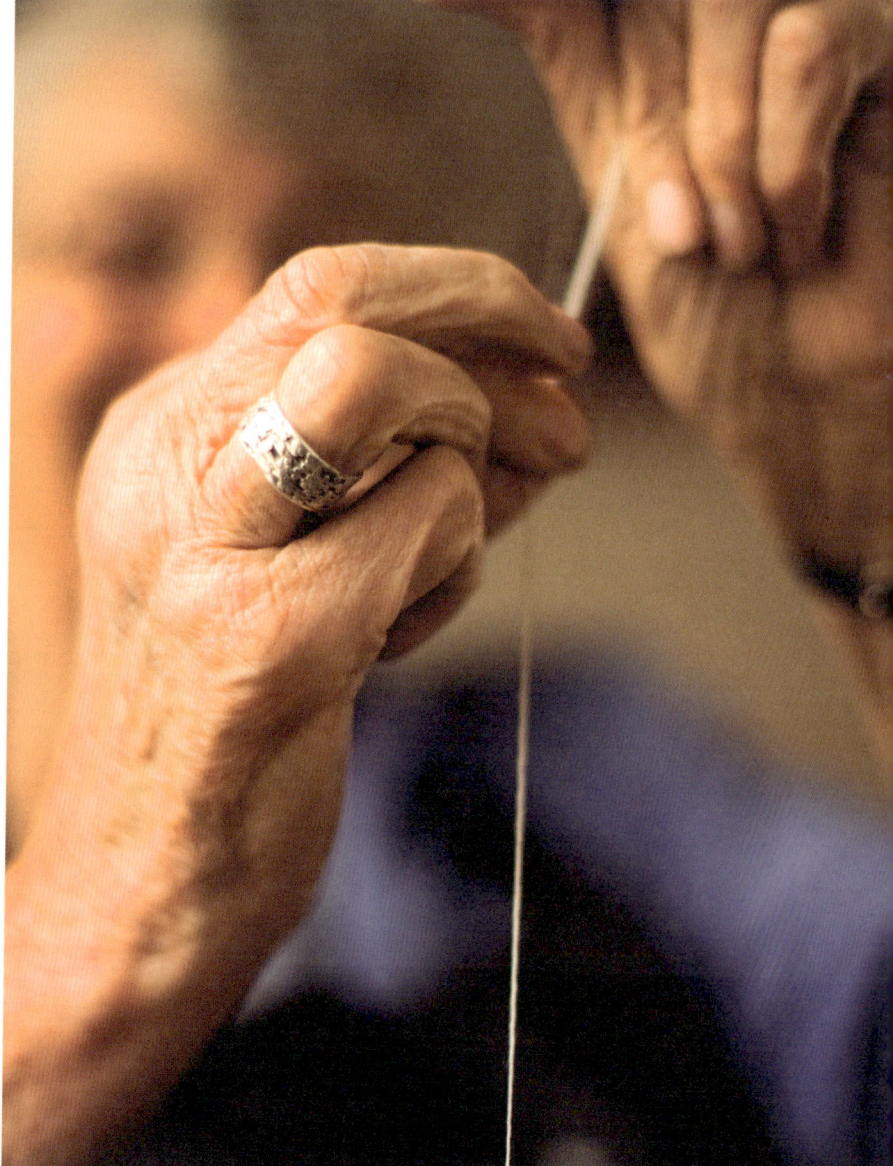

Kay Anderson, Spinner
Arbroath, Angus

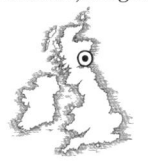

My name is Kay Anderson and I've been retired for 20 years. I have various hobbies and things that I do, and one of them is spinning wool.

When I first started spinning, which was over 30 years ago, there were only three people left in this county who could spin, and only one of them was really quite a serious spinner. But there is a long tradition of very high quality spun yarn in Scotland. Of course, there are still two places where the tradition of spinning has never disappeared. One is the outer isles —particularly Harris and Lewis— and in Shetland, which is well known for its wonderful work in wool.

Spinning is something which —it doesn't matter how long you do it— there's always something new, and someone to learn it from. However long you spin you're never really satisfied with what you're doing. It isn't just the spinning. You have to learn how to buy the best kind of fleece for what you're going to do, you have to suit the wool to what you're planning to make, and you have to learn to process the fleece of the sheep in such a way that you get a very nice spinnable material after all the works that you do. Then you spin it, and then you knit it, or crochet it, or weave it. But there is an almost infinite collection of choices which have to be made.

There are people —just a few— who, when they start to spin, it is as though their hands remembered what to do and it is as though they settled into something which they —a long time ago— have done. And that's a very great experience to be teaching somebody who has that natural affinity for it.

Bill Bontoft, Stickmaker
Manby, Lincolnshire

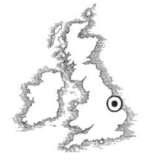

My name is Bill Bontoft and I was born in Lincolnshire, at a place called Binbrook.

My father was a rabbit catcher and always carried a stick, all his life. My stickmaking started with me scrounging at father for a stick and he would pull a stick out the hedge and say, "There you are boy, that'll do for now". As I progressed and got a little bit older and got my own pocket knife —and one thing or another— father said, "Well, you can get your own now boy".

I spent an awful lot of my life following packs of hounds. People saw what sticks I'd got, and asked me if I would like to make them one. About 20 years ago, I joined what is known as the British Stickmakers Guild. There are about 1800 members throughout the world. I make mainly working sticks not show sticks. Thumb sticks are made from antler and made from wood. I make knob sticks, I use buffalo horn, I use ram's horn. I do make traditional shepherds' crooks, for shepherds to use. Nowadays, the majority of shepherds use a metal crook that you can buy, but I still make them out of the ram's horn as they was always made, and people still use them.

I go out when the sap is at its lowest, normally about Christmas time. I collect all the sticks from the woods that are local to me and I leave them tied in bundles for approximately —well, I'll say at least 12 months— approximately 18, often two year, by which time they have to dry out. After that, you can then straighten them and pull 'em into shape. You work the top to make it fit your hand, or you join it to a piece of antler. Some of the times you can make a thumb stick, as opposed to the times you can make knobs. You can make whatever kind of stick you want really.

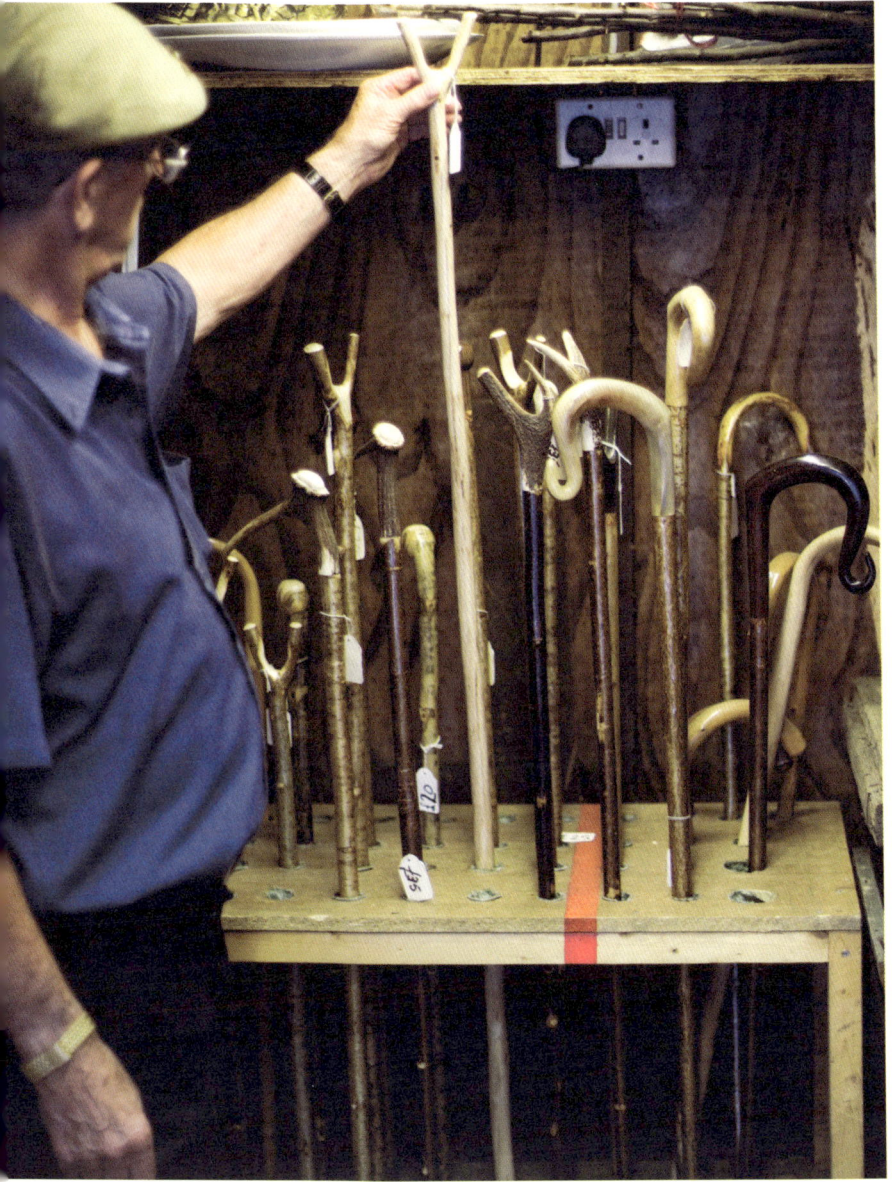

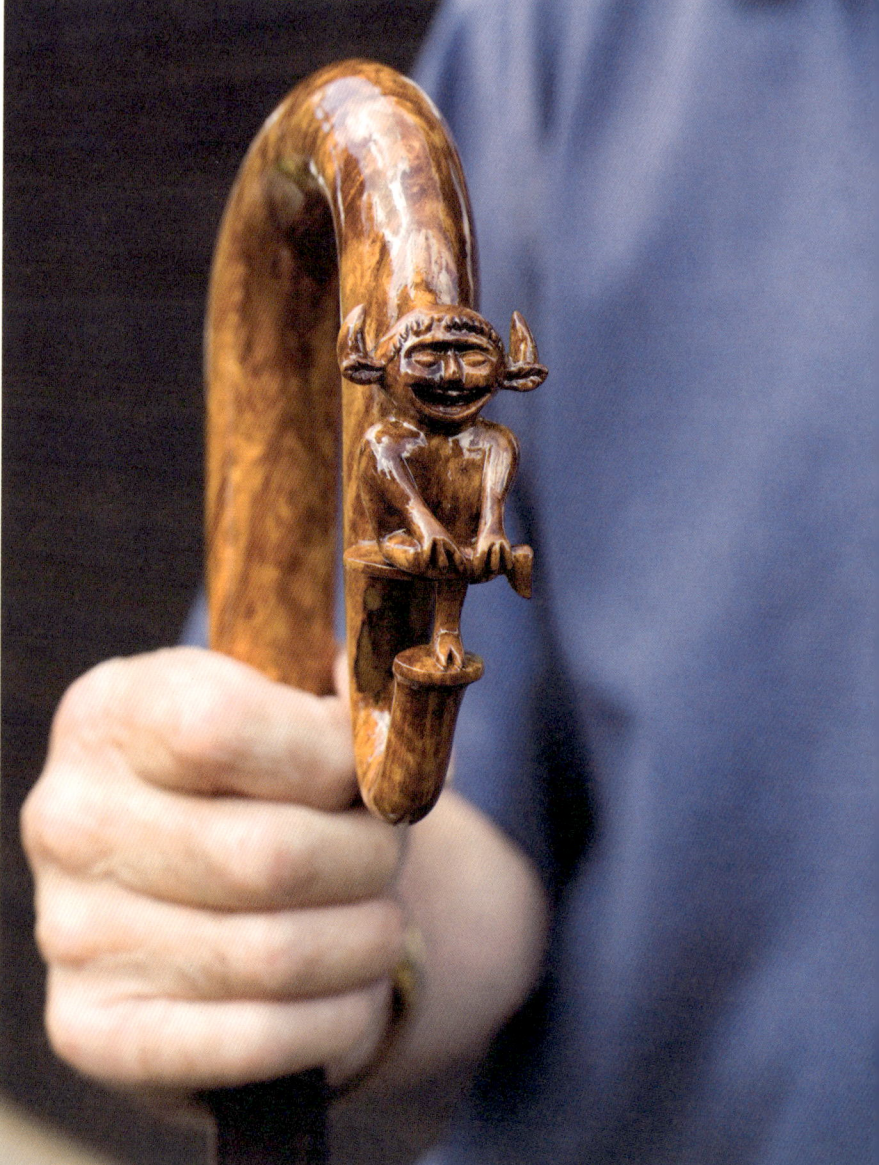

I've taught numerous people. The last person I really taught was a gentleman that lives in Holland. He comes to see me about twice a year. He was so thrilled that I'd done it. He could carve. He didn't know how to make sticks, but he was wonderful at carving. He and his wife came over about 18 months ago and his wife had asked him to make me a stick as a present for teaching him to make walking sticks. When he came over, he'd made a shepherd's crook out of wood and he'd carved the Lincoln Imp sitting on the nose of the crook — all out of one piece of wood. To my knowledge, there's two in the world: I've got one; and he's got the other and it is the most fabulous thing you could ever see. I'm so, so proud of that stick. I am.

I'm 72, and unfortunately I'm coming towards the end of stickmaking. OK, I've probably another 20 years yet —well hopefully I have anyway— but I love teaching younger people, showing younger people what I do. I do socialise with other stickmakers but, I'm afraid, there aren't many young people that are actually making sticks or becoming members of the Guild. We keep looking and looking and trying to encourage young people. That's my aim, to encourage young people to carry this tradition on, which would be fabulous.

Word-of-mouth, that's all. I'm 72 so I suppose there's a lot of years and a lot of mouth going around. I've never advertised at all, apart from just having a notice hung at my gate saying that I am a stickmaker, and they've gone all over the world.

Austin Brown, Bicycle Mechanic
Belfast

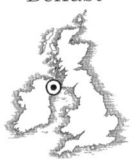

My name's Austin Brown. First and foremost, I would say —if somebody asked me what I do— I would normally say that I'm a bike mechanic.

I did a degree in environmental science at university in London and I worked for a consultancy quite a few years ago. I just got completely disillusioned with that whole side of things and decided to have a much more hands-on approach. So, I became a born-again cyclist in London at the age of 20 and I'm now 44. I decided to try to get as many people into cycling as I possibly could, because it's a terrific experience for a young adult to have that freedom in London, and then to do bike tours to get out of London and experience the home counties: Kent, Berkshire, Oxfordshire. It's a great way to see the world. Until I got a bike, I really hadn't left London.

Some ten years ago —more than ten years ago— I came back and I started a bicycle workshop here in Belfast. It was a shoebox size of a place in the city centre and it grew into a much bigger bike shop that would sell new bikes and lots of accessories and stuff. And I just became disillusioned with that whole side of things, there was more competition — bigger bike shops, much more flashy and stuff. At the same time, I got into the idea of teaching bikes and working with youth groups —maybe working with kids who are on the edges and fringes of mainstream society— so I started working with community groups here in Belfast, teaching young people different skills: how to fix their bikes, how to ride their bikes properly. I went to York and did a trainer training course to teach people how to ride bikes on roads safely. That was a week long and I came back. I'd incorporate the mechanical skills with the on-road cycling skills so people knew what they were doing with their bikes. If they did get a puncture, they could fix it instead of being charged 12 quid.

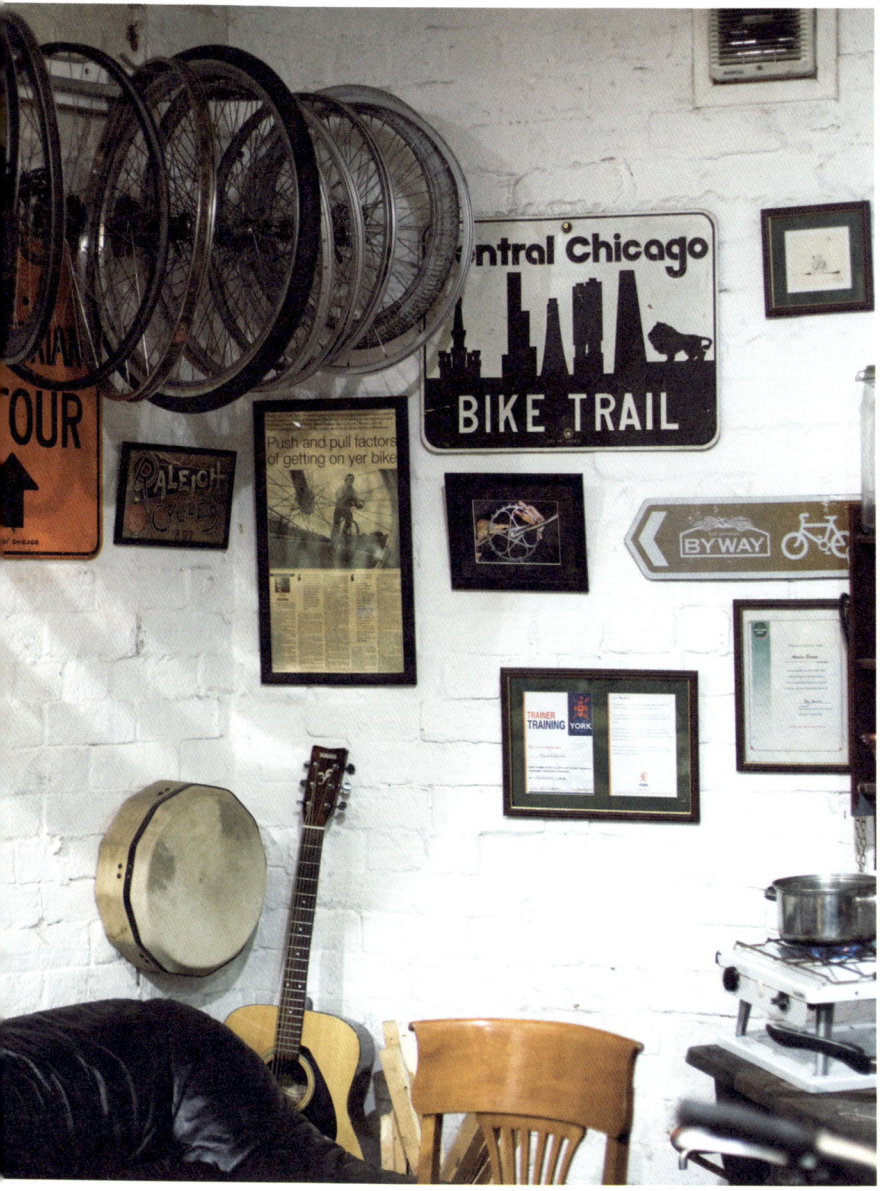

You know, a lot of families can't afford that sort of money. That's why a lot of bikes end up in back yards, back gardens, neglected. So I just wanted to teach people the skills they needed to keep them on the roads. More people on the roads means a better environment for everybody. I know governments talk the talk and really when it comes down to it, I don't see a lot being done here in Belfast. But we, here in the workshops, are walking the walk as well as talking the talk.

I do a lot of recycling as well. We don't sell any new bikes here, we sell all used bikes. We get bikes donated to us here. We're not a charity, I see myself as a social enterprise where we work on a social economy. Sometimes, I do a job for somebody for them to do another service for me. A plumber came in the other week. I fixed a couple of bikes for him and he's gonna to do a little job in the house for me. I like working like that. You know, cash doesn't have to cross palms, if you know what I mean.

I'm very interested in cycling —and cycling is what I do— but probably for the past five years, I haven't really done a great deal of cycling. I take a cycle tour —or two cycle tours— every year. I go to France, I did the Camino de Santiago, which I would recommend to anybody to do. I've done a lot of cycling here on the North West coast of Ireland, which I consider to be some of the best cycling in the world that I've come across, and a lot of other cyclists would agree with me.

Will Brown, Outfitter
Holt, Norfolk

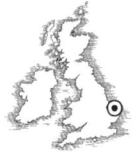

My name's Will Brown and I make clothes at Old Town.

We produce about 60 items a week that are cut out here, some of them are sewn here —we've got ladies who sew for us, there's seven of them— then the work's finished here, it's laundered, buttoned, packed and sent out from here.

If I was to describe the clothing, I would say it was workwear-inspired. Quite English or northern European workwear, as opposed to American, I suppose. I think it makes me laugh, actually. I think the most hilarious garment one could wear would be a khaki warehouse coat. It's just got sort of in-built comedy, which I like. There's nothing in the least bit flashy about it. It makes it look as if you're doing something a bit useful, even if you're not. It's very understated and quite comedy-worthy in an English sort of way. The other day, I thought that if you took sitcoms from the seventies, it's sort of all there. It's Arkwright's warehouse coat in Open All Hours, or Granville's Fair Isle slipover. It's those comedy clothes that I quite like. It's sort of aspiration but in an odd direction. Like the sort of people that you'd admire would be engine drivers or coal miners.

I'm very much inspired by things from quite a broad period. I like those 19th century catalogues where you get the illustrations of two men —generally arm in arm— wearing a lounge suit or something. But that's also part of the idea, it's got reference points that are historical, but the idea of them in a modern garment is quite strange. And that's the fun that you have with them really.

For many years we tried to keep it exclusively British fabrics, but it's harder to maintain that. Woollens isn't much of a problem because you've got Harris Tweed. We get serge —which is like bus

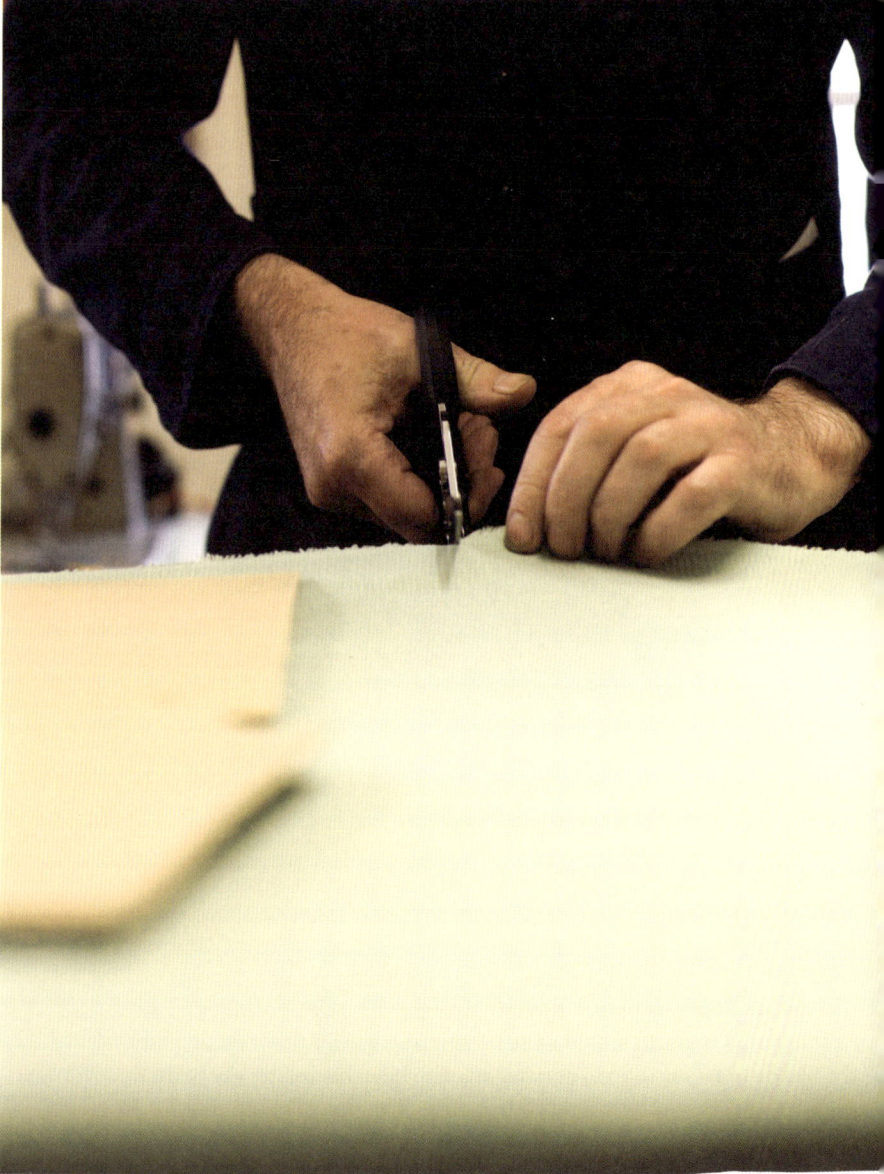

conductor trouser material— you can still get that woven in Yorkshire. And Irish linen. So all that's left is cotton, that's the difficult one. I don't think there's anywhere that still weaves cotton in this country. There's a heritage mill in Lancashire —a steam mill— the chap who works it does demonstration lengths of striped cotton shirting. So he can get 30 metres to us every couple of months or so, but I think that's probably the only British woven cotton. The cotton drills —which have still got their austerity numbers classified by 31/10 or 31/11, they're still called by those names— I think they are woven in India, but it's quite likely they're made on the machinery that was exported from Lancashire, so there's still that connection.

The prospect of making the business bigger appeals on one level, in that one wants to get the things out there more, but it would be almost impossible to make it much bigger. I suppose that the way that we work, and the way that it's made with a four to six week lead time on delivery —and the experience of often making the journey to Holt— could account for about half of the appeal of the garment. And if it was just a rack of shelving where hundreds of other identical items were, then obviously it wouldn't have the same appeal. I think people do like that aspect of it.

I would like to design more clothes but, because it's very hard to remove anything from the range, it does creep ever bigger and one's aware to keep it as quite a tight product. But it would be nice to design more clothes, that's the bit that I like doing best of all, just seeing whether something new will work.

Merlin Crossingham, Animator
Bristol

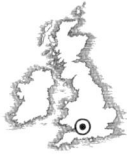

My name's Merlin Crossingham and I've worked for Aardman for nearly 14 years.

I came here straight from film school, where I studied animation. I had no intention really, of working for a big company. I was going to be a sort of fine art film maker, who made fine art films, and suffered for their art, and was penniless. Somehow, Peter Lord —one of the founders of Aardman— saw my showreel, saw something in it and asked me to join an apprentice scheme to train animators for Chicken Run, which I joined and never left. I've really enjoyed it, it tapped into something. Performance really challenged me — getting performance from characters on a stage. Getting puppets to act and to express themselves really tickled my imagination and really challenged me in a way that I found immensely satisfying. I just tried, and tried, and tried to be as good as I could be at animation —character animation in particular— and so that's what I set about doing, and this is a brilliant place to pursue that. So I stayed, and I ended up working on both of Aardman's big feature films and all the other high profile Wallace and Gromit jobs. And now I'm directing Wallace and Gromit, so it's been a very nice progression into that.

The core of it, though —originally for me— was the craft. The craft of learning the skill of animation to such a level that, on your bad days, your craft skill is going to keep you going and make your work really quite good. And on the days when you come to work and your creative juices are flowing, your craft skill and your creative inspiration link up and make your work blinding. And that's what we rely on. Our benchmark for everybody across the board —from animation, through to set dressers, and directors of photography, and everybody who's

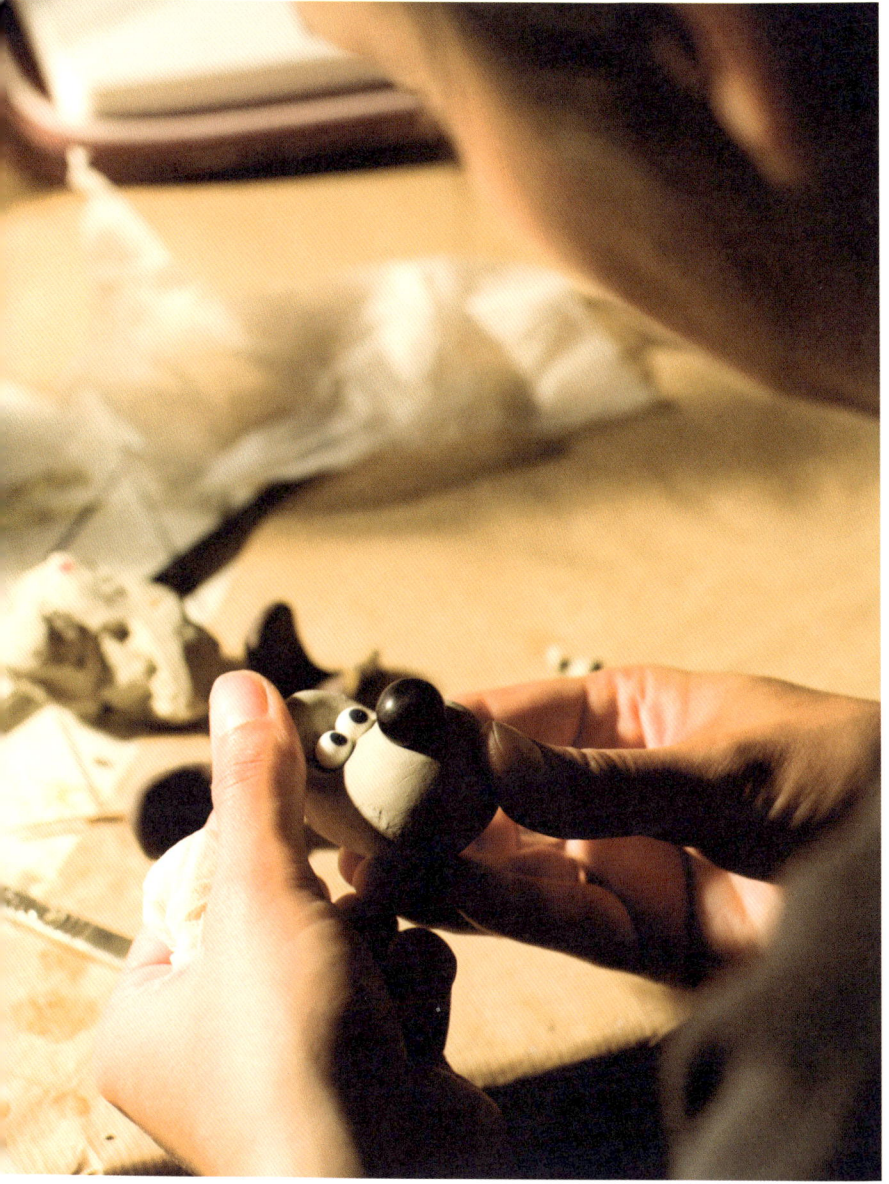

working— is that the base level of craft skills is so high that, when they're having a bad day, it's still better than most other people and, when they're having a good day, it's just amazing.

I think, if you enjoy what you're doing —in whatever craft it is— that keeps you going. I think most crafts, at their heart, are a passion. I don't think you can get a high level of craft skill —be it stone masonry or sculpting plasticine or whatever it might be— unless you're truly passionate about it. If you're not passionate about it, you're not going to put in the hours, and the weeks, and the days, of practising and refining and getting to the stage where you don't actually consciously think about it. It's like when we see new animators coming through, you can tell when they're "getting it", because they stop asking questions. They stop consciously thinking about the decisions they're making. When they stop thinking about the technical aspect of animation, they start thinking about the expression and the performance. So you can clearly see it in a young animator, as they take the lessons from each day and log them in their animation library. It equips them to be able to focus more and more of their energy into the actual performance of the characters.

The Wallace and Gromit humour stems from Nick really, they so much come from him in every respect. Originally, it's things that made him laugh, and things that he found amusing, and references that he thought were clever, witty or funny. Wallace and Gromit sort of mirror the success of Aardman. You know? They make things in their basement and slowly they've got bigger and bigger until they had their own Hollywood movie. And Aardman's the same. It started in a garage, two guys sort of inventing it as they went along. Now it's a brand in its own right. Curious parallels but I think they do go hand in hand.

Sheena Devitt, Stone Letter Carver
Lochgilphead, Argyll and Bute

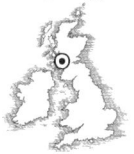

My name is Sheena Devitt and I'm a stone letter carver.

I'm from Northern Ireland but I came over to Scotland in 1985 to do drawing and painting at Edinburgh College of Art. But I always felt —when I left college— that I wish I'd had more of a design or craft training. You know, just that craft side — making something.

In the eighties, craft was definitely a no-no. Nobody wanted to be associated with it and then in 2003 —well I'd been doing calligraphy at night classes for a few years before that— but in 2003, I got a chance to go down to mid-Wales and study one-to-one with a master letter carver and do an old fashioned apprenticeship for three years with him. That's given me a real grounding in a particular craft, which I feel very grateful for. In 2006 I moved back up to Scotland and just knocked on a few doors, and found this space. Well, the guy I rent it from helped me make a space within this scrap yard, but it's absolutely grand, you get a great sound —when it rains— from the tarp. It's just mostly word-of-mouth and my website that bring the jobs in. I've got a little kiddie, so I just work on a part-time basis at the moment.

A huge part of the training was learning to draw letterforms so you don't need to look at anything. You can recall the letterforms and start to invent your own, based on classical forms, just from your head. You can always look at reference books around you, but I think it's a bit like a classical music education, you need to have all that solid training, then you can improvise afterwards, or it tends to look a bit fuzzy.

For good letter carving you need a real tension in the design for it to have impact, basically. You can see over there. That would be a design that is based on classical letter forms, but I've adapted it.

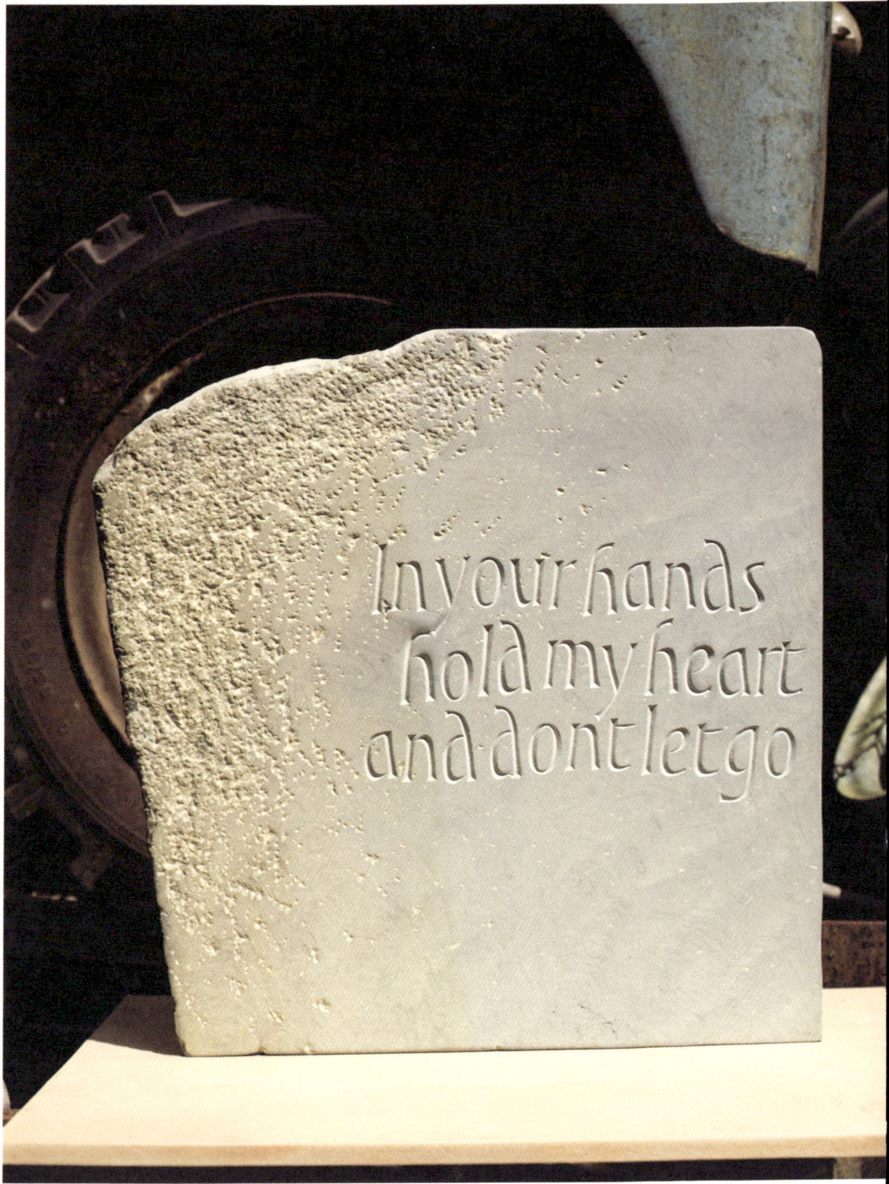
In your hands
hold my heart
and dont let go

For example, it doesn't sit on a straight baseline. The client wanted something quite informal, and some of the letters join up to echo the meaning of the words. So, it's a little bit like a jigsaw, you have to keep moving the letters around. The layout is really important. The layout is just as important as the letterforms, and it's the kind of thing where millimetres matter, so you have to be a bit fussy.

I can be quite scattered in my head and to do letter carving you have to be completely focused. The combination of that 100 per cent concentration you need, and working with a physical material like stone —which is solid— it literally earths me, and I think it just keeps me balanced. The other aspect I love is, I love playing around with light. The difference between, say, doing calligraphy on a piece of paper and carving into stone is that it's a v-cut which captures the light —especially if you light it from one side— it's like capturing light in stone. So those two things are what makes me passionate about doing it.

When you're working for a client —especially when you're doing something like a memorial— when you go through the process of working out a design with them, at a very poignant time in their lives, and then you go to fix the final piece of work —either in their garden or a memorial site— it's a very moving and privileged process to be part of. These are the things that really make me love doing what I do. And to be able to earn a living from it is very lucky.

Martin Doyle, Flute Maker
Liscannor, County Clare

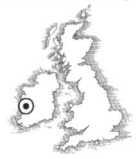

I'm Martin Doyle. I make flutes in Liscannor in County Clare, in Ireland.

At the moment, myself, I'm playing an eighteenth century flute. It's one I made myself, it's a copy of an eighteenth century flute and I really like the tone of it.

As time went by, the volume came up and the holes in the flute got bigger. The tone got stronger and more equal. The older flutes, some notes were strong and some notes were very weak, then there was a way of playing it, you made the balance up within yourself. Where, in a modern flute —if you take the latest, like a modern bone system flute— all of the holes are the same size. They're big. An equal sound comes out of every note. I think those old instruments are very beautiful, I think the sound from them is exceptional. The oldest instruments had a very small sound which grew in the environment. Where a modern flute almost has a sound inside itself, do you know what I mean? So it's an "in-your-face" sound.

There are different stages of making. When you're doing boring and reaming and things, this is very physical and fast-moving work, but when you come down to where you're putting keys on the flute, it's very quiet, small work. You can spend a lot of time here in the quiet. It's a nice feeling. You can walk out of the workshop really slowly at the end of a day. You know? It's kind of satisfying.

Well, there are so many sides to it because when some young person comes in and they pick up a flute and they make this music, you know that they've got something good to work with, you know that they've got something — they can develop it. You know? You know also that they've got something that they can give to their grandchildren. And they're only ten at the moment.

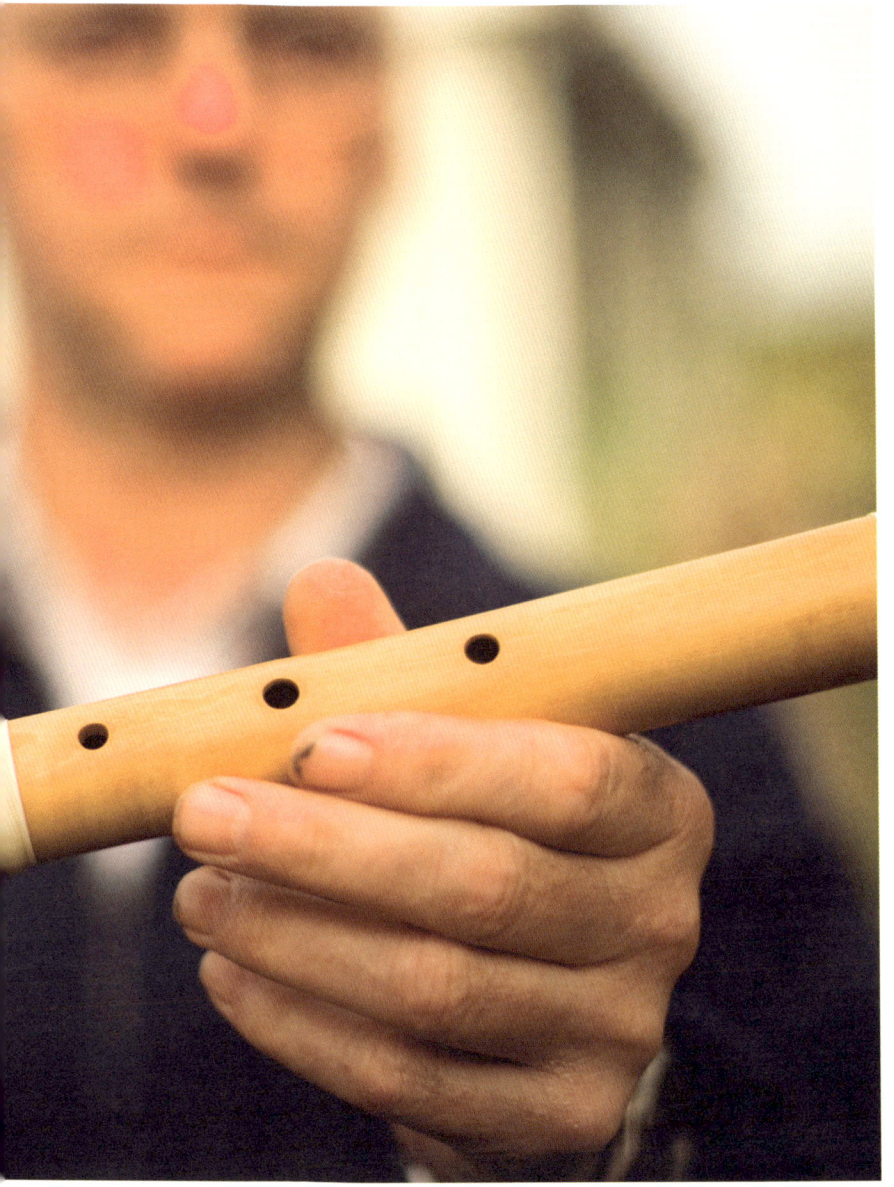

Laurence Edwards, Sculptor
Butley, Suffolk

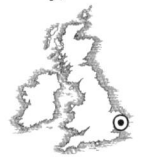

I'm Laurence Edwards and I'm a sculptor. Residing in Suffolk, Butley. Butley Mills Studios on the creek. I principally work in bronze. I have my own foundry and I share and run a studio set-up here, with about 13 other artists.

   It's very rare that I get the opportunity to make a statement in landscape. This is an ongoing project — they're three, eight-foot figures in bronze that have been made from the materials of the landscape. So they've been made with mud from the marsh, and all the reeds around here. Ostensibly, they are one figure that has evolved. So, one big clay man —or mud man— was made, and then a mould was made of him, he was cast into bronze, and then the clay that was left was turned into the next man. And he was bronzed, and the next man came out of that. The interesting thing about that is that a physiognomy and a build stayed with these figures, and they end up looking related. It's something I stupidly hadn't really thought about. Making an almost indigenous person, I suppose, or a person that sort of relates to landscape. A physiognomy and an eye, and a way they stand —or the way they look in triplicate— gave them a presence and a power. They started to tie in with the history of this place —the whole Saxon history we have here— and also the contemporary world that exists here as well, the music that exists.

   On one side of me —on the left hand side— is an international concert hall started by Benjamin Britton. And on the right hand side, is Sutton Hoo. And in the middle is this creek, and I like to think of myself in between those two places. So to position myself in the landscape in that way —sort of metaphorically, or intellectually, or whatever you want to call it— has given me a real anchor to this landscape, and the fact that I come from here as well, really helps. But basically, it was how was I going to tie in that idea, and how was I going to use the landscape and make the connection good and proper.

I decided to make a raft —almost like a little island, a little piece of Suffolk— and transfer and sail these figures up the river. I decided to make a journey to the Aldeburgh festival last year. So they sailed up the river from Aldeburgh to Snape on a big, sort of symbolic, voyage. They were positioned outside the concert hall, in the reeds, floating on the tide. So they raised and lowered with the tide. They were in concert —'scuse the pun— in concert with the landscape, where they were almost like barometers that chronicled the weather, the conditions, the tidal heights. So they fused with the landscape in a really interesting way for me and gave me a lot to work with. Out of that, films were made and we made a book that recorded the project. It was wonderful.

I had a big commission and I didn't know if I could do it. I thought, "I'll try a figure out first, in this scale with my foundry", which is a very small foundry. They were cast in 12, 13, 14 pieces and welded together. Because of that, it became a piece of personal archaeology, because they were destroyed and then reconstructed. I was almost destroying myself and then reconstructing myself in bronze, in a funny sort of way. And that journey —because they were really about me and for me— was quite extraordinary, because it was the breakdown of a person and the build up of a person at a certain time of life through a landscape that I cared about it.

It was an arrival in many ways for me, and it was reaching a plateau in life where I felt like it was great to have really engaged with a piece of landscape on a personal level. To return back to working

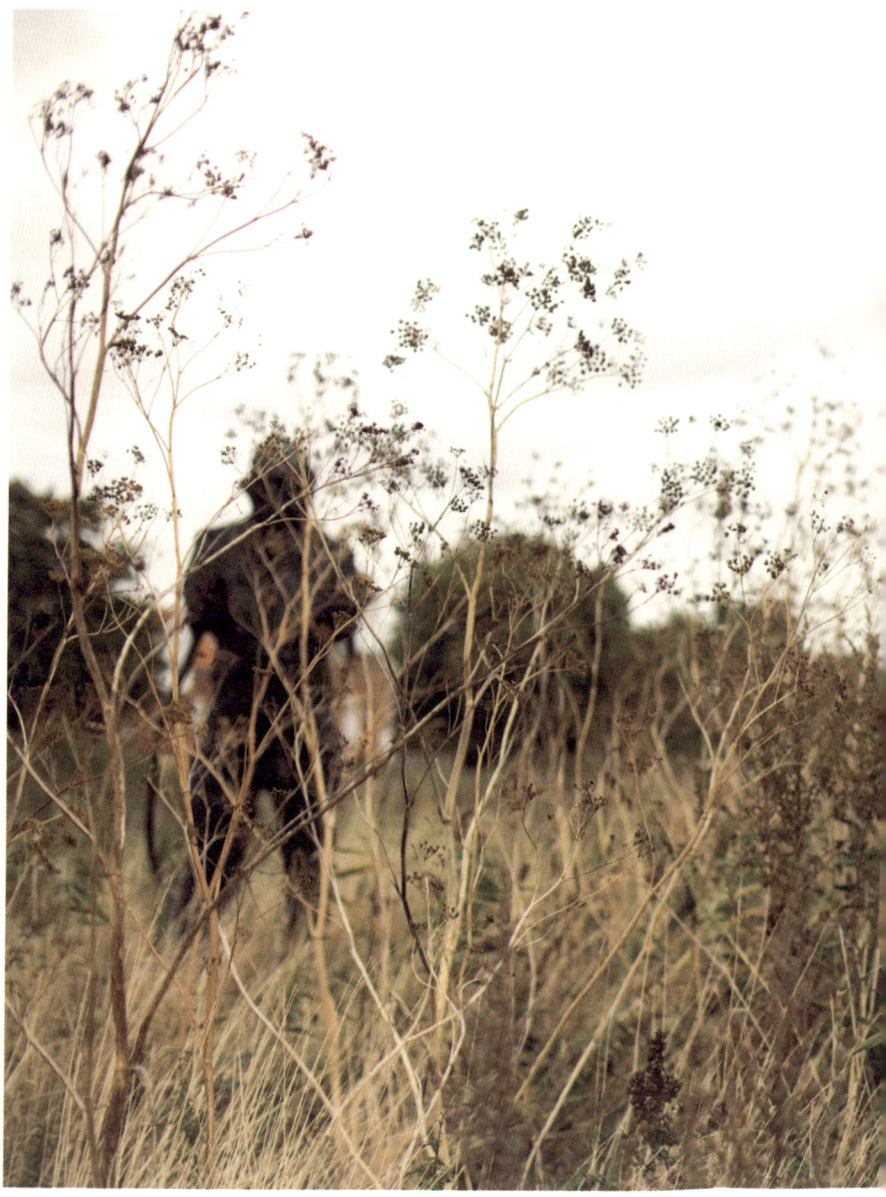

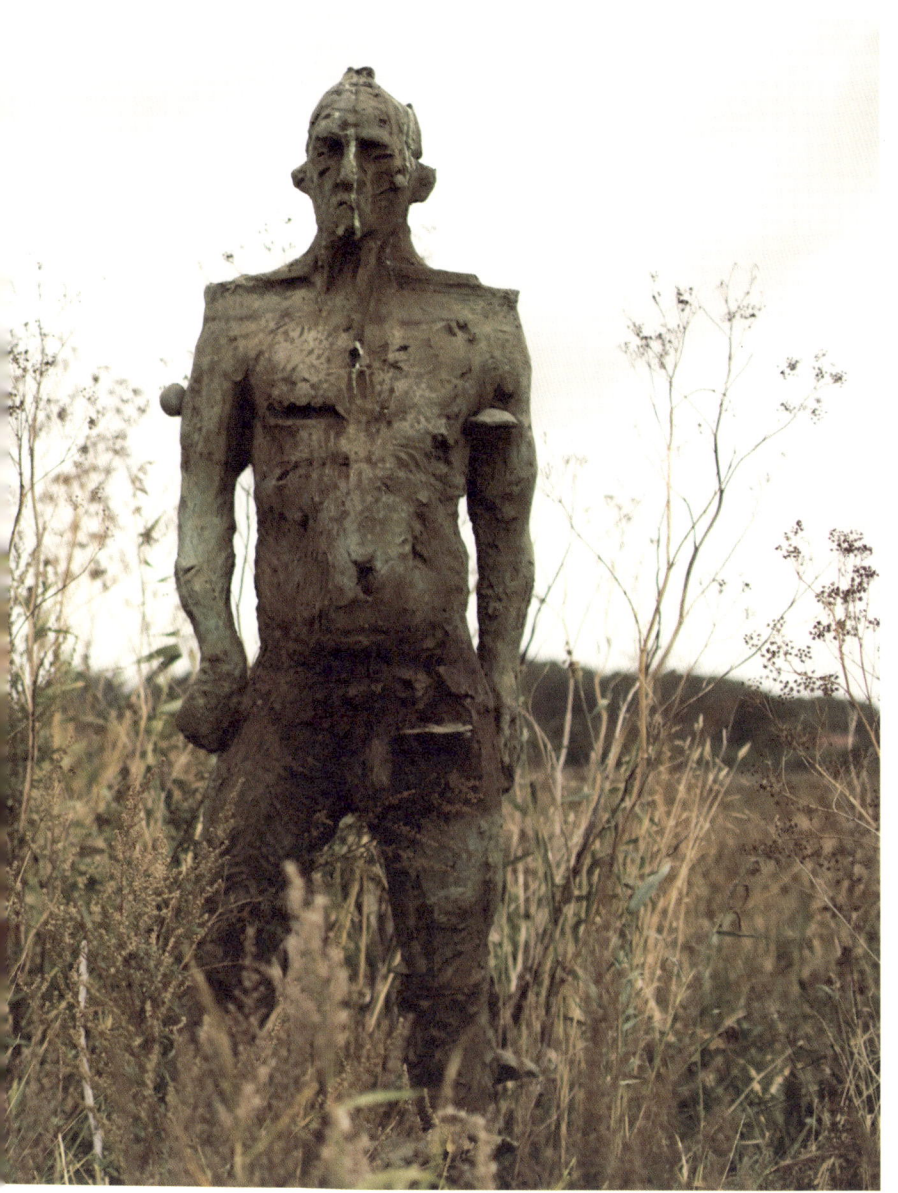

professionally as a sculptor after that —with commissions and stuff, which are brilliant and great fun to do— it slightly dimmed all that experience in a funny sort of way. But again, to look at it in a more positive way, it forces me to be confident enough to put more of myself into the commission work that I do.

So I think as a result, my work, and the galleries that I work with, probably feel a more confident artist coming out, a person who's much more happy to talk about himself and put himself forward. So that's what it's done for me. I've crossed the Rubicon. Literally.

Douglas Grierson, Weaver
Edinburgh

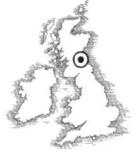

My name is Douglas Grierson. I'm head weaver at the Dovecot Studios. We weave tapestries and we do tufted rugs.

It arose really out of the arts and crafts movement. William Morris is one of the stalwarts of the philosophy behind the Dovecot. So that's where it started. The fourth Marquess of Bute, at that time he took on the mantel of setting up a studio in Scotland, in Edinburgh. Two weavers from William Morris' workshop at Merton Abbey came up to start it off and train apprentices, and that's how it started. Unfortunately, the two of them were killed in the First World War. So that was from 1912 until, I think, one of them eventually left to go to the front in 1916 and was killed within a couple of weeks. Then the apprentices came back and took it from there. So there wasn't really that much training for them, they had to literally pick up the threads again.

In the twenties, they wove hunting scenes and historical tapestries for the various houses or whatever the Marquess of Bute had. After the Second World War there was a change. There was a move to more modern tapestries, maybe more domestically sized as well. After the war, we had Stanley Spencer, Graham Sutherland... artists like that. They did a whole series of tapestries by the most modern British artists at the time. That kind of legacy has carried on to this day. Although there's weavers' work done, the bulk of the work is through artists.

I suppose it's a sort of growing thing. When I started as an apprentice I didn't know anything about tapestry. It became a kind of vocation at the end of the day, you know? Because you've got tapestry studio weavers numbers dwindling over Europe. France was the place where there were most tapestry studio weavers. Then in the sixties there was the explosion of tapestry artists.

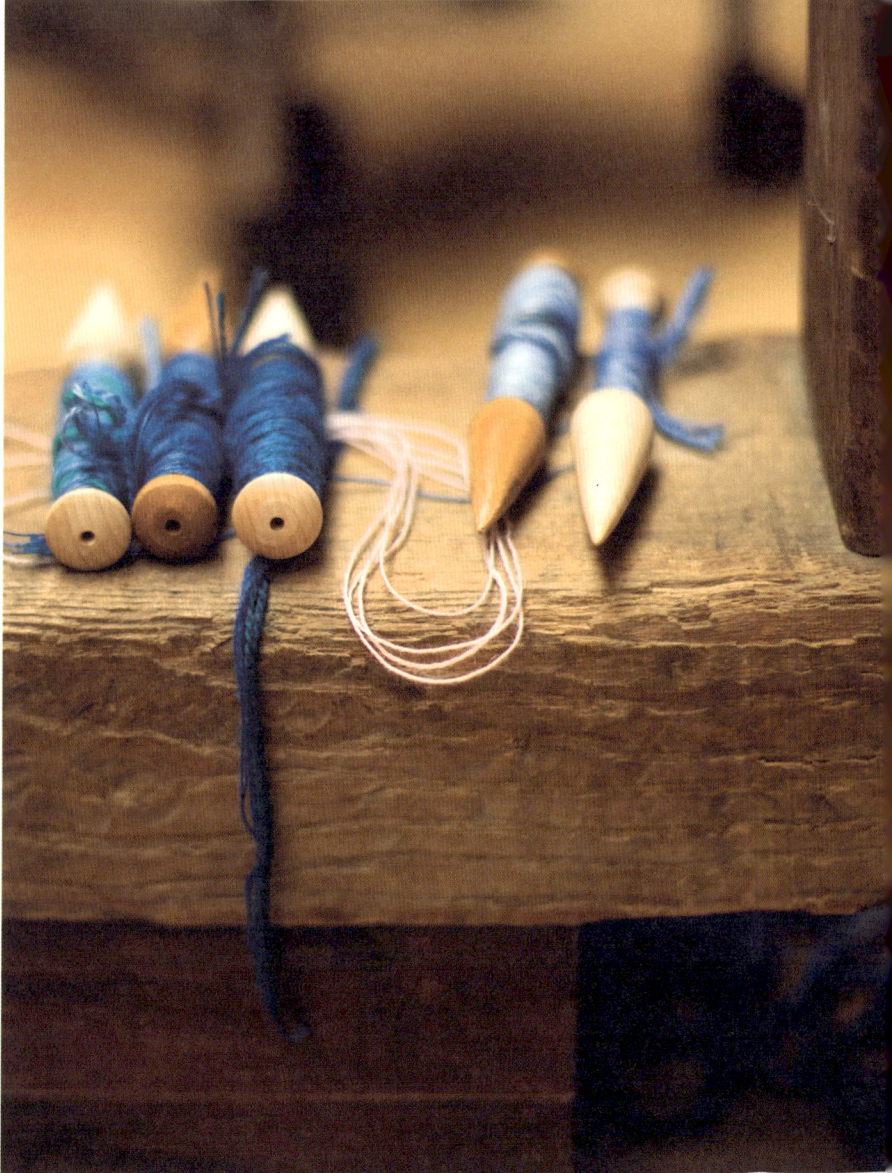

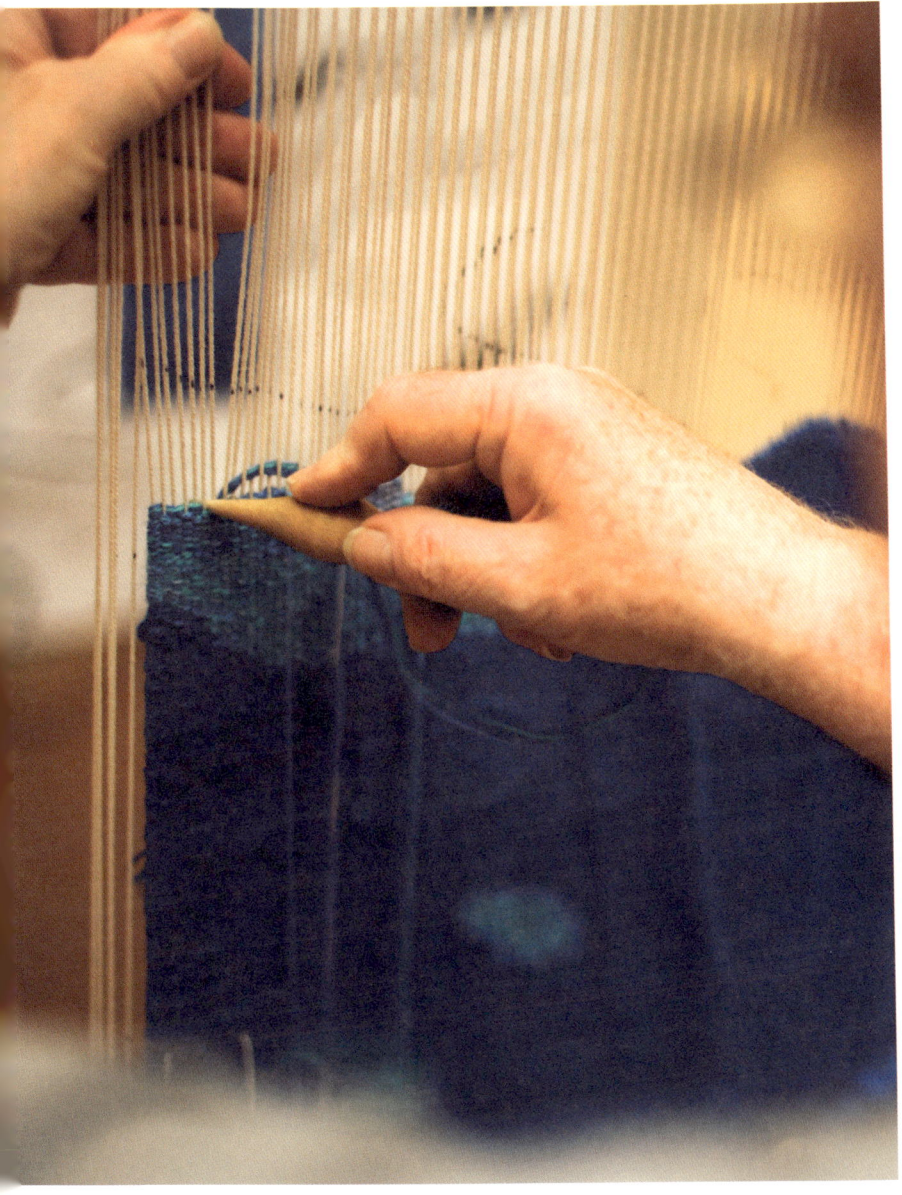

This is when it became, not studio work, but artist weavers. And, of course, that evolved as well. So now you've got the two. You've got the studio work that we do, and artist weavers.

I like the idea of keeping the studio alive and keeping it going, because it is different. I mean, working with other weavers is what I like. I've done it sitting alone and weaving. A craftsman's life can be lonely when you're doing whatever you're doing — if you're doing it for other people and you're in your studio.

It's a kind of way of life and it's something that we all love, because weaving's a lovely thing to do. You know, it's quite relaxing and it's a bit therapeutic. It can be hard work as well, because a tapestry can take a long time. You can be sick of the sight of it by the time it's finished, on some works. And some others, you get surprised that you've woven it and it's got a life of its own.

What I like to do is to work with the artists. Having the artists in here, working with them, showing them, because it's a learning process for us as weavers working on an artist's work. I think the rapport between the artist and the weaver shows in the tapestry at the end of the day.

John Joseph Hanna, Hat Maker
Donegal Town

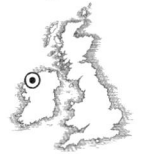

John Hanna. John Joseph Hanna. Born and bred here, in Donegal Town. Born on the 13th of March 1944.

My father came from Belfast. You just mentioned you cycled from Belfast, well you're the second man I know who came to this factory from Belfast. He was born in 1905, dad, and when he was 19, he answered an ad in the newspaper where there was a position for an apprentice tailor. Wrote, got an interview. So he left Belfast on his bicycle on a Sunday morning, because he worked six days a week.

He was born an orphan boy, and was left on the doorstep of an orphanage when he was only six hours old, in Belfast. The Convent of Mercy nuns, they reared him until he was six years old then they handed him over to the Christian Brothers, who gave him his education. When he was nine and ten, if a button fell off their jacket, he would ask if he could sew the button on. So, from a very early stage, he was showing an interest in garments and traditional trades and tailoring. When he was 12, when he got a summer holiday, he used to work as an apprentice tailor for a company called Clarks on the Falls Road. When he left school at 14, then he went down and got a job full time with this company. But he left that company when he was 19, and came to work in Donegal Town for a tailor here. He never left Donegal after that. He married my mother when she was 19 —he was 27— and they had 11 kids, seven girls and four boys.

The trade has continued on and on since then and it's now in a third generation. My father died in 1985. On the 10th of October of this year, I'll be 50 years in Hanna Hats. It's a long time. A lot of buttons sewn on.

Heads. Heads is the most special thing. When my father was being interviewed back in 1973 by a reporter from one of the national newspapers, he said to my father, "Dave," he says, "How long do you think these hats will last?" And his reply was, "As long as people have heads". But, together with that, it's to be innovative, to be creative. New designs of tweeds, new colours of tweeds. There's changes of the hat and cap, the style has changed dramatically over the years, from the walking hats and walking caps and country caps.

See that hat there? A young guy of 18 years of age. Right? He's dead now. He became attached to the World Banking Federation of Ireland. His father brought him in here for a hat when he was going to university when he was 18 years of age, and he wore it all over the world as a fishing hat. Three years before he died, he came in here and he gave it to me as a present. He says, "Your dad made that for me." And that hat was one of the first ones we made.

Hanna Hats are in love with the product and I think that's what has kept Hanna Hats here. It's a dying type of tradition — it's something that we've inherited deeply within ourselves that is inescapable. You just cannot get away from it. It's the love and desire to create and design something and take it out to a show and see someone say that they'll have a few dozen. And then it explodes from there, into different shops and mail order houses such as L.L. Bean, Freeport, Maine, or Bond Street in London, or Paris, or Germany, or Japan. That's the drive. The drive is passion. And pride. When you take all the heritage that you were born with —it's in your blood— and you carry it on, that's the driving force. But if you haven't got the respect and love for the garment and the tweed —to nurture and put it all together— then you ain't going to go anywhere. I think that has died in a lot of companies in Ireland, and England, and the world over. That's what has died.

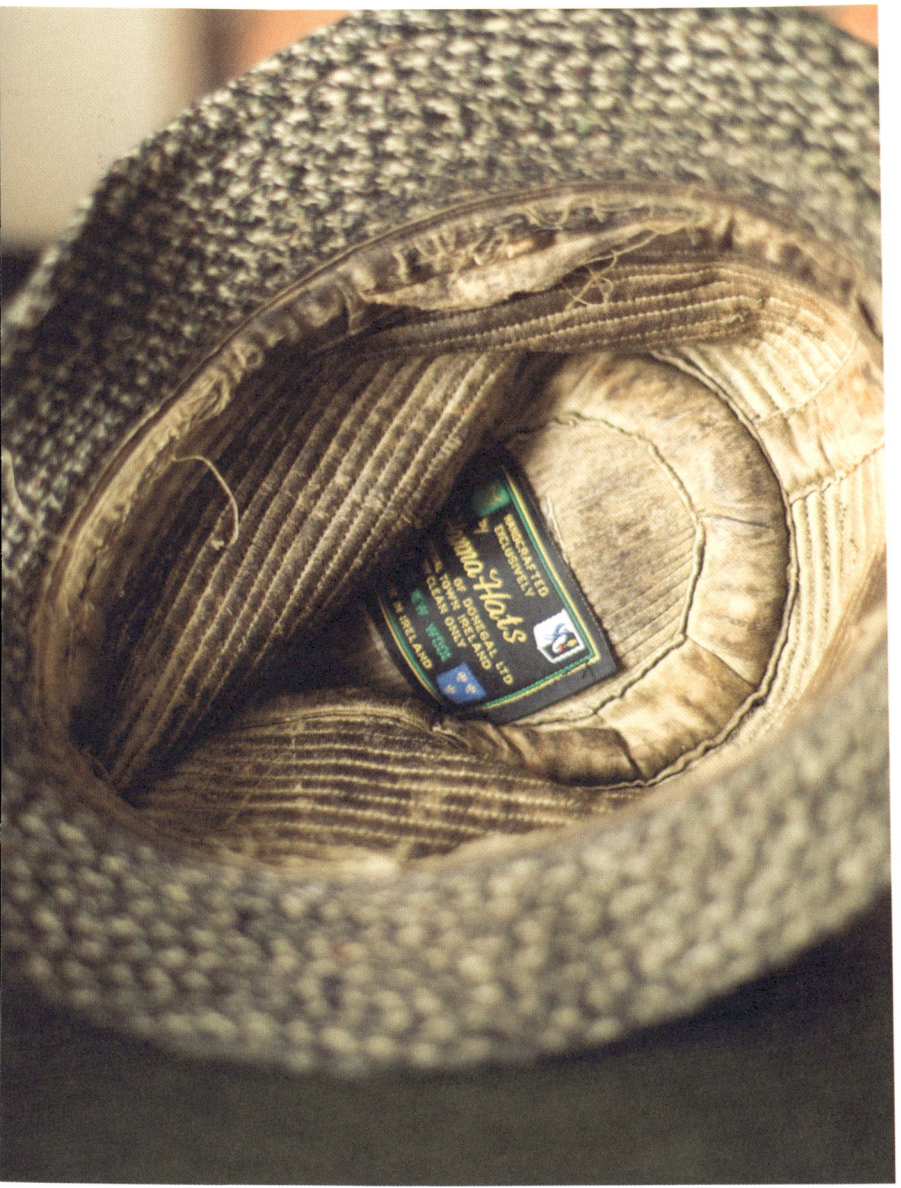

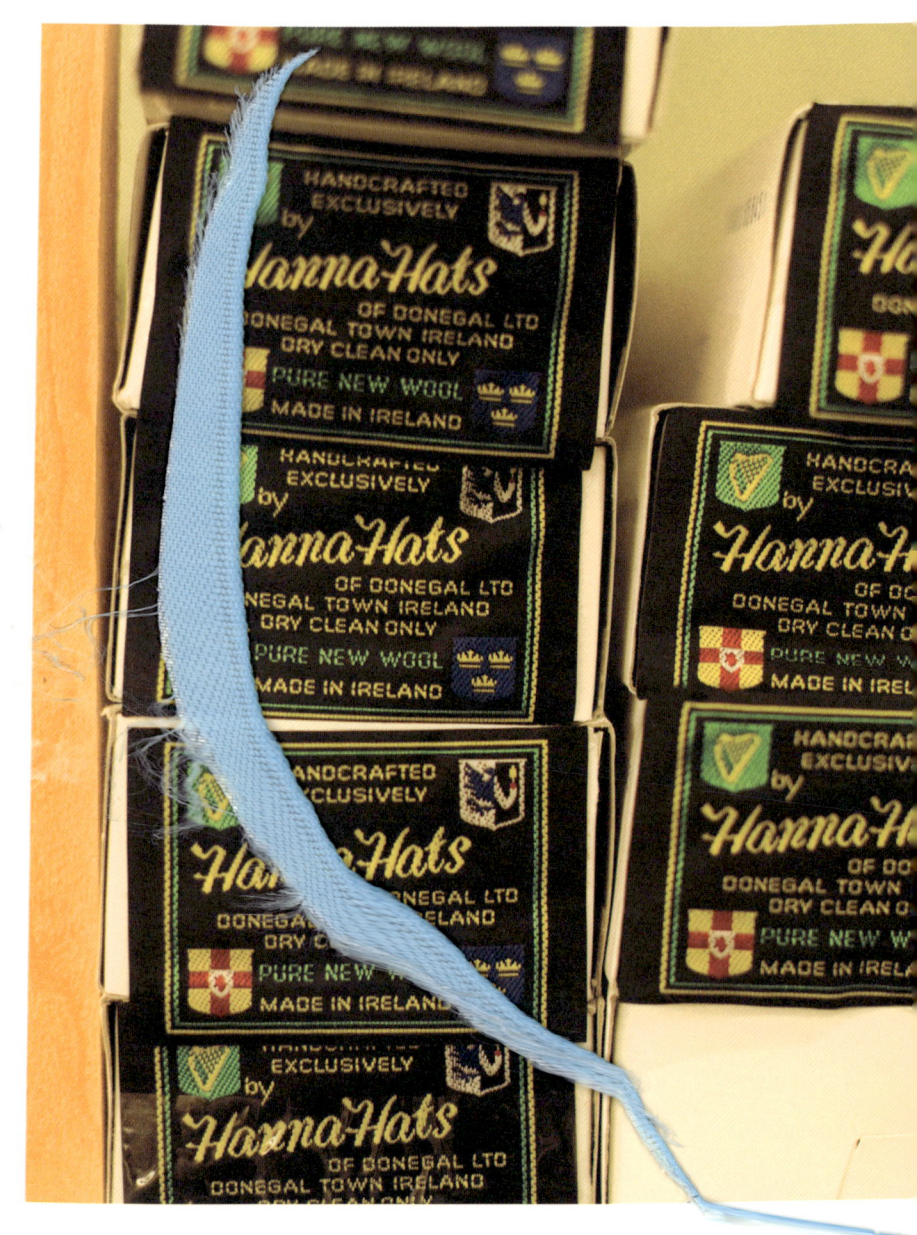

I think, if small and medium-sized companies —who have had that in the past can re-light that, ignite it again and get that drive, and passion, and pride, then there is a great vacuum there in the world today for great products that come with that pride. But the passion will be seen in the finished product. There is a market there for it. I think it can be re-established, and employment can go on the up-scale, if we can instill that in the minds of people again.

Joanne B Kaar, Paper Maker and Artist
Dunnet, Highlands

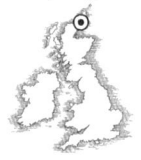

My name's Joanne Kaar. I'm a paper maker and I'm from Caithness.
I live just up the road from Mary Ann's cottage and I've been fascinated by this place for quite a few years. We're sat in Mary Ann's cottage at the moment. This place has been in Mary Ann's family for about 150 years and they didn't throw anything away. It's a traditional crofting way of life. So, it's now open to the public and it has been left as if Mary Ann is about to come back, all her stuff, the chair set out as if she's been sat by the fire and just gone out to get some peats.
I started drawing every artefact in the cottage and I went off and did other projects. Starting to look through my sketch books, I thought about what to do next, and I'm fascinated by a sea chest that is in the cottage and there's a painting of a ship, the Westland. The sea chest belonged to Mary Ann's father, William Young, and he was a crew member on the Westland's maiden voyage in 1879. It sailed from Scotland to New Zealand, and I've been following its voyage and I've linked up with an artist in New Zealand, Lynne Taylor, so we're both obsessed now with the Westland ship. She's been studying life for immigrants as they arrived in New Zealand, in Port Charmers, and I've been studying the life of the crofter and William's family, here in Dunnet in Caithness.
After I've done my drawings, I start to make artefacts. I've been starting to experiment with paper using different fibres that I find locally so, as well as making things from horse hair, I've been using heather, I've been using grasses, anything I can find that might have been used on the croft. I've started to make imaginary things that William might have had in his sea chest, so I've made a paper jacket from peat. So it's peat paper. You can actually wear it, it's adult size. I've also

made other things —studying the voyage of the Westland— a log book following the same 80 days as the voyage, documenting the ships in the Pentland Firth. Lynne in New Zealand has also done a log book to follow the same 80 days.

One of the passengers on the Westland wrote a diary —Jonathan Moscrop— and one of the particular dates in the diary was an event that happened on the 27th of February 1879, and it marks one month into the voyage. Once the crew members signed up for a trip they were paid a month's wages in advance. It's kind of a contract. So, for the first month at sea, the sailors feel like they're working for nothing. The Captain is said to be "flogging a dead horse". It's not really true, they've already had their money, they just have to work for it now. So, after one month they have a ceremony and they call it Braying the Dead Horse. On the Westland —from the diaries— I know that the crew —which William Young would have been involved in, Mary Ann's father— they made a horse from string and a piece of old pipe. They auctioned it on that day, and in the diaries it tells us that the highest bidder was five bottles of whisky, so I think they got very drunk. They set fire to the horse and threw it overboard, and watched it going into the distance. So that's where the saying "flogging a dead horse" comes from. I've imagined that those five bottles were also tossed overboard, and I like beach combing, so I've collected five bottles from Dunnet beach and made labels to do with the ship on them, and I've also made a very elaborate string horse.

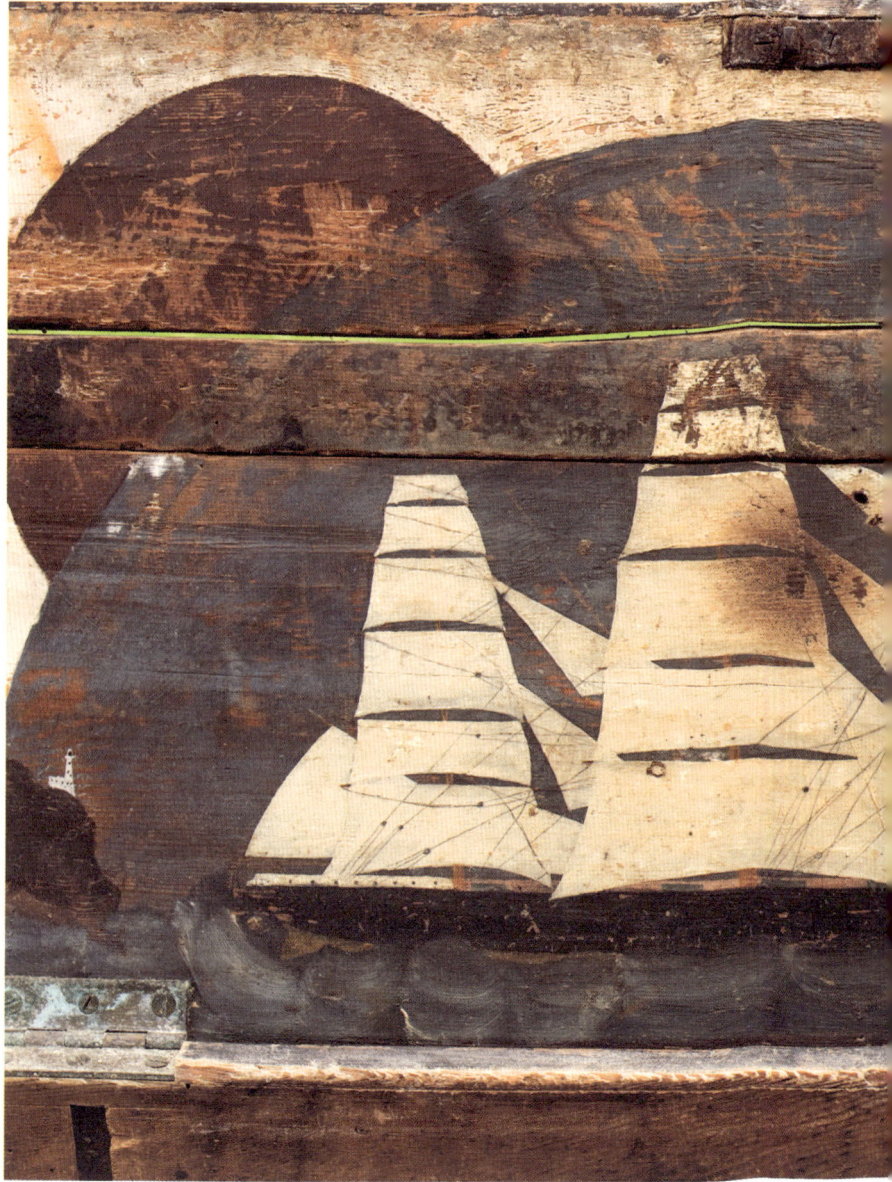

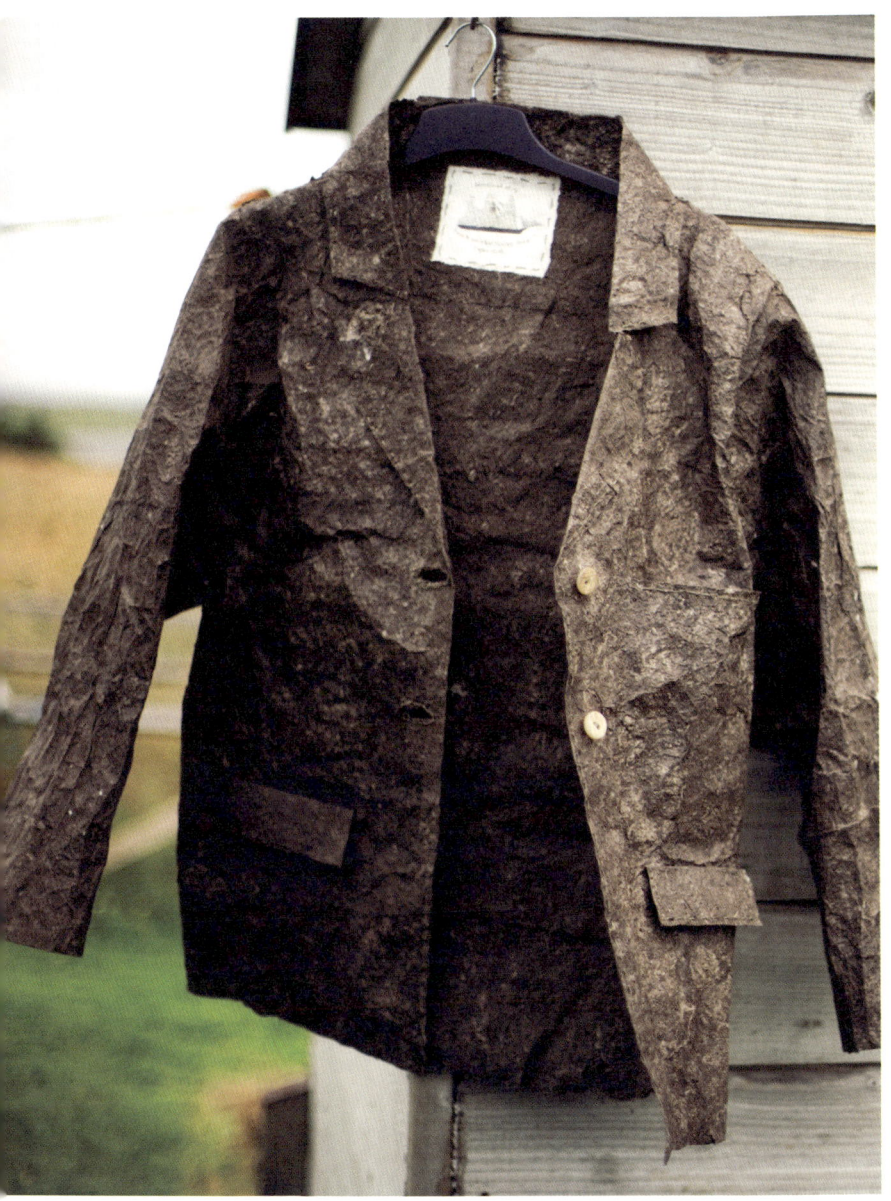

Paul F Kelly, Gold and Silversmith
Kenmare, County Kerry

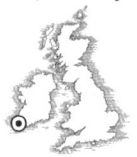

Paul Kelly, Gold and Silversmith. We're based here in Kenmare, have been for nearly 13, 14 years. I'm a mussel farmer as well.

The mussel farm tends to be busy around January, February, March. That's when we start harvesting mussels. The jewellery shop tends to be busy from May, June, July, August and then, after that, you're quiet for a bit and then you're getting ready for Christmas. That's busy with the jewellery as well. So the two of them work hand-in-glove fairly well together. Because this is fairly precise, intense, indoor work, it's lovely to have the contrast then of the boat and the physical, and the harvesting the mussels, and the growing the mussels, and being outdoors. So you get the best of both worlds, if you know what I mean. You get the pleasure of sitting in here making stuff, and then on a fine day —like today now, this evening— you could go out on the boat, and harvest some mussels and have a nice barbecue.

I was very lucky to get an apprenticeship in Kilkenny with a guy called Rudolf Heltzel —who's a German master craftsman— and with Peter Donovan, who is an English Silversmith. Between the two of them, I got a fairly rounded work experience in the metalwork, both silversmithing and goldsmithing.

You know, it probably sounds corny, there's something terribly satisfying about sitting down with a blank piece of metal. I was never really very good at fine art when I looked at it closely, so I can't really sketch something out, you know? Or come up with a design on a piece of paper. It's more... you sit down with a piece of metal. What I very much like about this craft as well, you know I'm a craftsman, first and foremost — although every now and again I like to think of myself as an artist. But, I'm actually just like a plumber, a shoe maker or a carpenter.

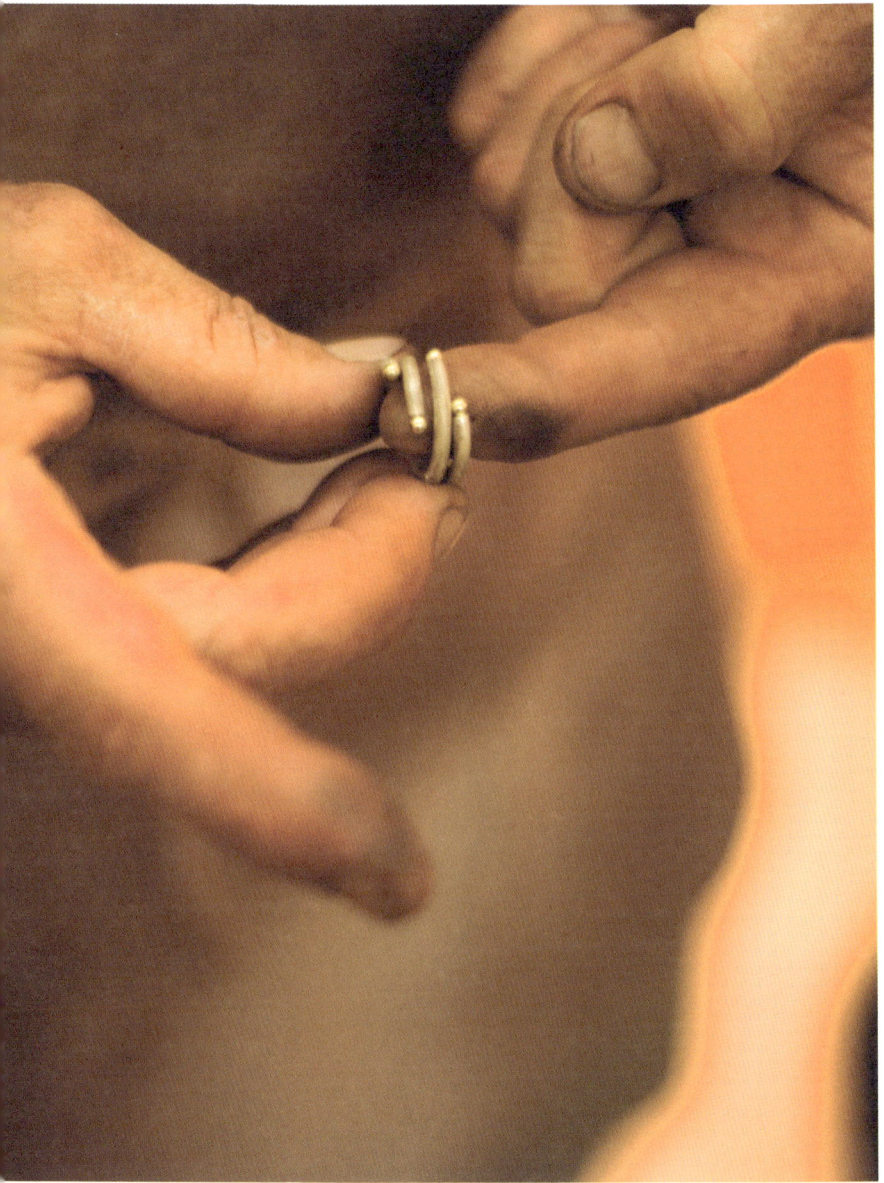

So, when I want a plumber I ring the plumber and when the plumber wants a wedding ring, or something for his wife, he rings me. So, I mean, it's a trade and you wouldn't want to be taking yourself too seriously now, and getting arty-farty. It's a practical skill that you can learn, and you can teach to somebody else.

So, with that in mind, when somebody comes in and requires something, to be able to sit down with a piece of metal and try and figure out from them what they want, and try and offer suggestions — you know we're like an architect and a client. And then, if you do that well enough, that then gives you the time and the money to buy more metal, so I can create my own pieces that I put on display and someone comes in off the street —a tourist or a local— who isn't looking necessarily for anything, but likes my work sufficiently to part with their hard-earned cash. You know, a lot of my pieces —it's 18 carat gold, it's precious and semi-precious stones— it's by no means cheap, it's quite expensive because it's hand-done and I value, and appreciate my input, so I charge well for it. But somebody who doesn't necessarily need a ring says, "You know, I love that so much I'm going to buy it". That's what's incredibly satisfying about it. You know? Honest to God. Seriously. It sounds a bit corny I know, but that's the greatest kick I get out of it.

Nigel Legge, Fisherman, Artist and Lobster Pot Maker
Cadgwith Cove, Cornwall

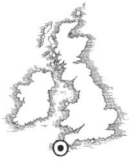

I'm Nigel Legge. Fisherman, artist and willow lobster pot maker.

I was born in 1950 and I was brought up in Cadgwith, a little fishing place, by my father, a fisherman. I used to go out with him in a boat. Then —at the age of 17 or 18— I joined the Merchant Navy for seven or eight years, and came back. I saved up 1200 pounds in the Merchant Navy and I could have bought my grandmother's thatched cottage for 900 quid but, instead of that, I bought a fishing boat and the next year the house prices went up, and I never actually caught up with them anymore. But then it don't really matter, it's dead and gone now.

Now, as I'm getting older, I'm doing a lot more painting, making pots, willow lobster pots. As I get even more decrepit, I can probably sit up in my little studio with the sun shining and paint some pictures of fishing boats, and reminisce of years gone by, and just probably be a pain in the neck to all the young fishermen when I want to go to sea once in a blue moon.

At this very moment, I'm as fit as I've ever been. I discovered yoga about three years ago and I recommend that to any old codger, it just keeps you stretched. I'm not seizing up, and keep working. Retirement, stopping, is just a nonsense really. OK, not kill yourself through work, but just keep doing a few bits and pieces and stay with the youngsters. Don't join too many "old" things, the youngsters actually keep you alive, really, and they're brilliant. Most youngsters are actually brilliant. They get a very bad press a lot of them, but most of them are as good as gold and, treated right, then they're OK.

Lobster pot making I learnt when I was 14 or 15 from my father. These days, everybody thinks it's a marvelous craft and how clever you are, and everything else, but it's nonsense really because years

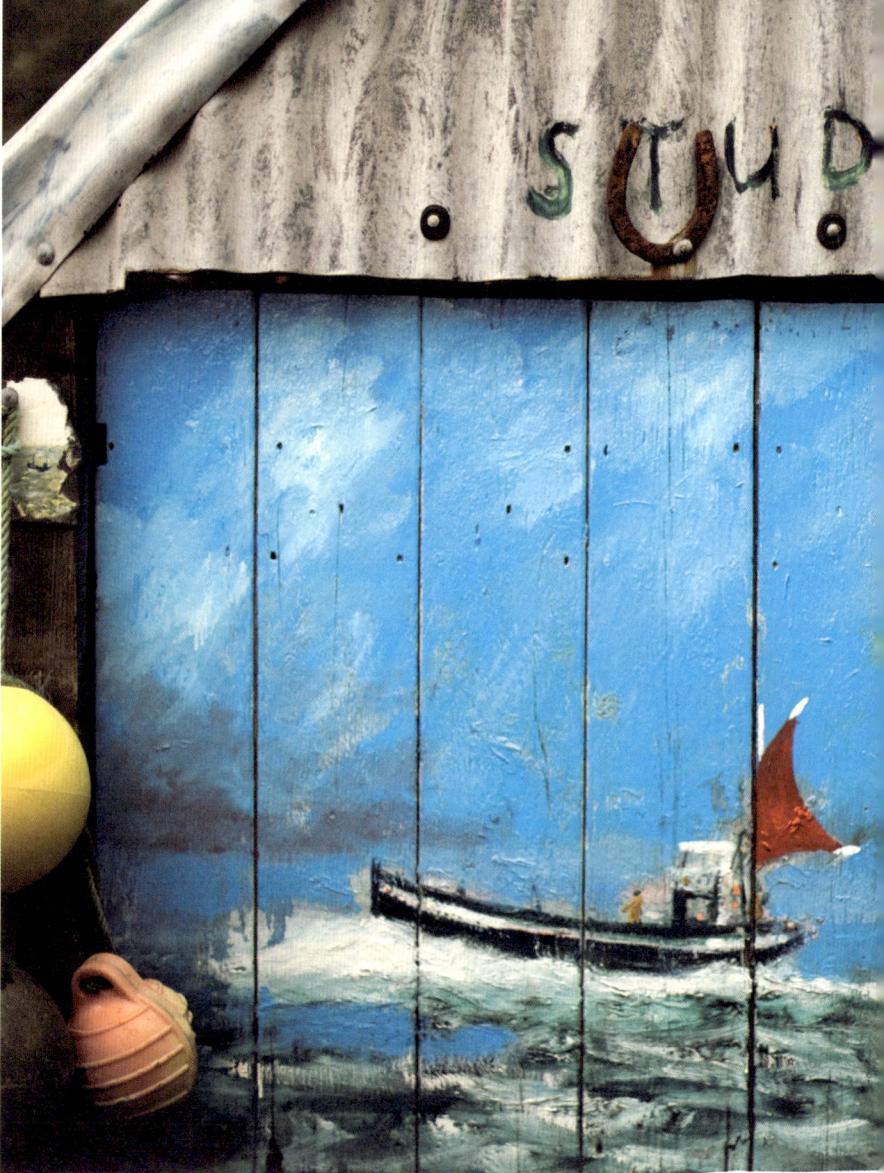

ago you had to make lobster pots to go crabbing and lobstering, or else you didn't go because you couldn't buy steel and plastic ones. I used to hate it years ago because it was hard work. I actually quite enjoy it now. It's a bit arty-crafty now, and all the rest of it, but I enjoy it. I only make lobster pots, I don't make baskets or anything like that.

Well, the fishing... I suppose, being a fisherman, rightly or wrongly, it's what sells the paintings and the pots. People have got this romantic thing about fishermen —which is total nonsense— but, when they see the cove, and the boats, and the sun, and the lovely fine weather, I suppose it is semi-romantic. I have got to say now that the pots and the paintings help me to carry on fishing, because it's not so good as it used to be, but the fishing sells the pots and the paintings. So, it's just the whole... all jobs together are one, really. Just one big bowl mixed up.

The beach is the focal point —and the pub and the cove— for anything that's going on. When I was a boy, the thatched cottages were slums. There's no mistaking that. The toilets were a bucket and chuck it down the beach, there was no running water, and the rats ran through the cottages with hob-nail boots on. It was a rough place. That all changed when they put the mains drains in, and electric. People had a very, very hard existence, same as everywhere in the country, I suppose.

People make it special, really. You get quite a few people, who've moved down, and the ones that integrate with the locals actually give the place a boost and help it to keep going. I wouldn't like to live in Cadgwith or Cornwall with totally Cornish 'cos it would drive me bonkers, to be quite honest. But, with a good mix, it's pretty good really.

Dominique Lieb, Letterpress Printer
Dingle, County Kerry

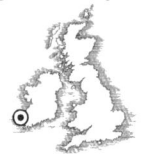

My name is Dominique Lieb. I'm from Switzerland, from Zurich.

When I came here, I got into contact with a man who ran this letterpress here in Dingle and he told me that he wants to sell it. My plan was just to stay for a year, but then something in the family happened —and my daughter went to a school that was very good for her— so I somehow decided to take over this press, and to stay here. As far as I know, Púca Press is the only letterpress still working. There is a museum in Dublin and they have a kind of letterpress, but it's a museum.

In the first year or two, I was mainly doing business cards, letterheads and invitations. But somehow the jobs got a bit less. There is also a copyshop in Dingle, and he's a bit quicker. Through learning Irish, I got into contact with some very special people: farmers mainly, and poets. I found out that they are very good speakers. I decided, if I do books —like these small books I have here— I like to have the Irish language in the books, because this is somehow an exchange. I do the images and somebody would write the text. If it's in Irish then something new would somehow come out of it, and this is my main interest, to mix these two cultures. The work process is very slow. It is labour intense. When I would set these words —these Irish texts— so slow with the letters, that would help me to learn the language.

It's handmade and I don't mind if it looks handmade. It should be done carefully, and it should be clean, but I like this plain look. No plastic and no gloss. You can really choose the paper —the material is more important— then you have content, a story and images. It's just different, I believe.

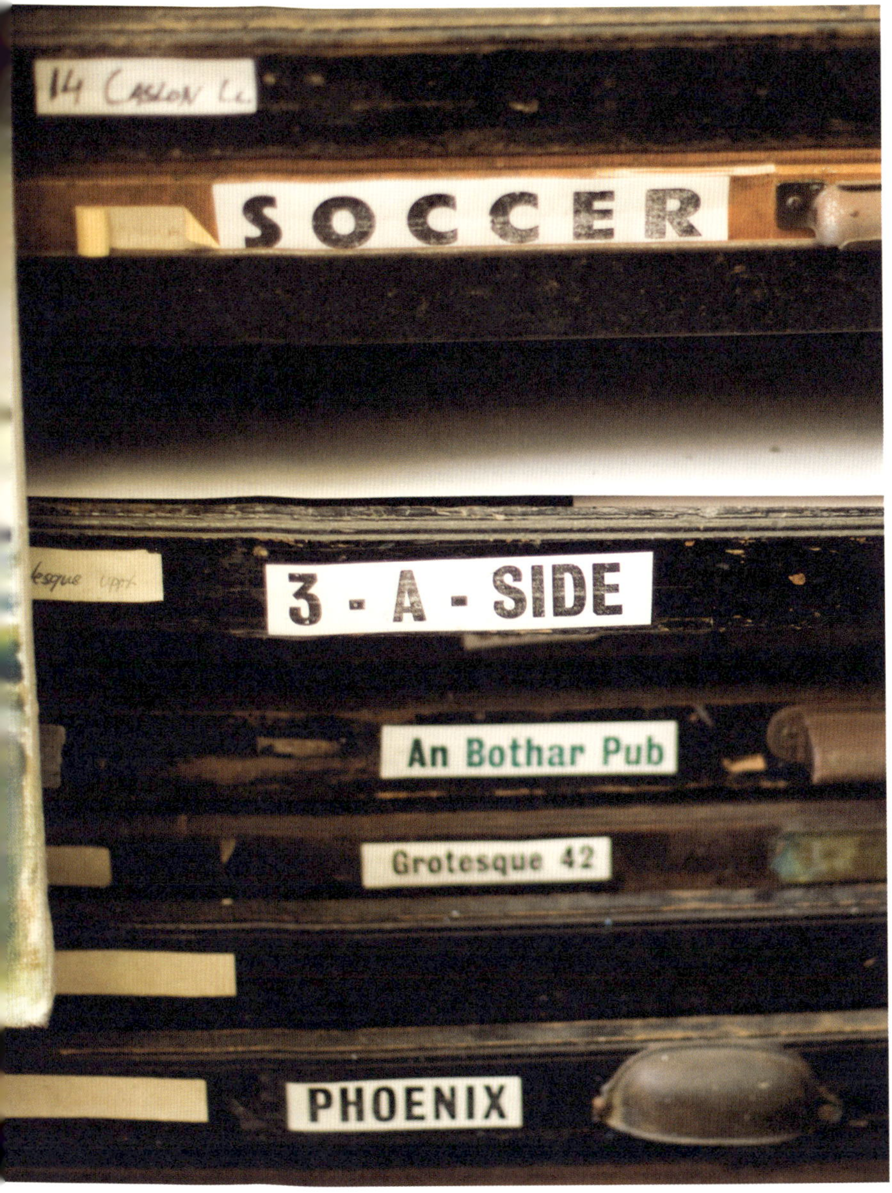

14 CASLON L.

SOCCER

3 - A - SIDE

An Bothar Pub

Grotesque 42

PHOENIX

Joanne Mitchell, Glass Maker
Sunderland

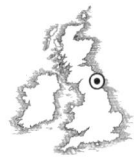

My name's Joanne Mitchell and I'm a glass maker.

I did a masters degree in glass product design and I became a designer for Edinburgh Crystal, up in Penicuik near Edinburgh. I worked there for a couple of years, and then decided to set up my own business and produce my own personal work. That led me down here to the National Glass Centre where they had a scheme for start up businesses, and I got an incubator unit —which is a tiny little office in the centre— and I've been here ever since. The business has grown and I've started in business with Jessamy Kelly —three years ago now— doing the fuse glass. So, I've got the two businesses now and we work together sometimes, and we also do our individual work as well. There's so much around to support glass makers. There's a network called Cohesion —there's about 120 glass makers just in this area alone— and there's a history of glass in this area, as well, so it's a real hub of activity and that's why I came back here to start making my own work. St Bede came over in, I think, the seventh century. He came over and brought stained glass window makers to the area. So there's a history of stained glass in the area. In fact, St Peter's church —which is just around the corner— had the first stained glass windows in the UK, so I think that's where it started. And then —obviously through the industrial revolution— there were glass factories built here. Unfortunately, the industry is pretty much gone now, but these individual makers and craftspeople have continued working.

It's a difficult material because, to grind and polish it, you have to go through five or six stages. A lot of it has to be done by hand as well, there's no easy way to work with glass. It's got to be annealed well, if you don't anneal it properly it can crack, so that's something

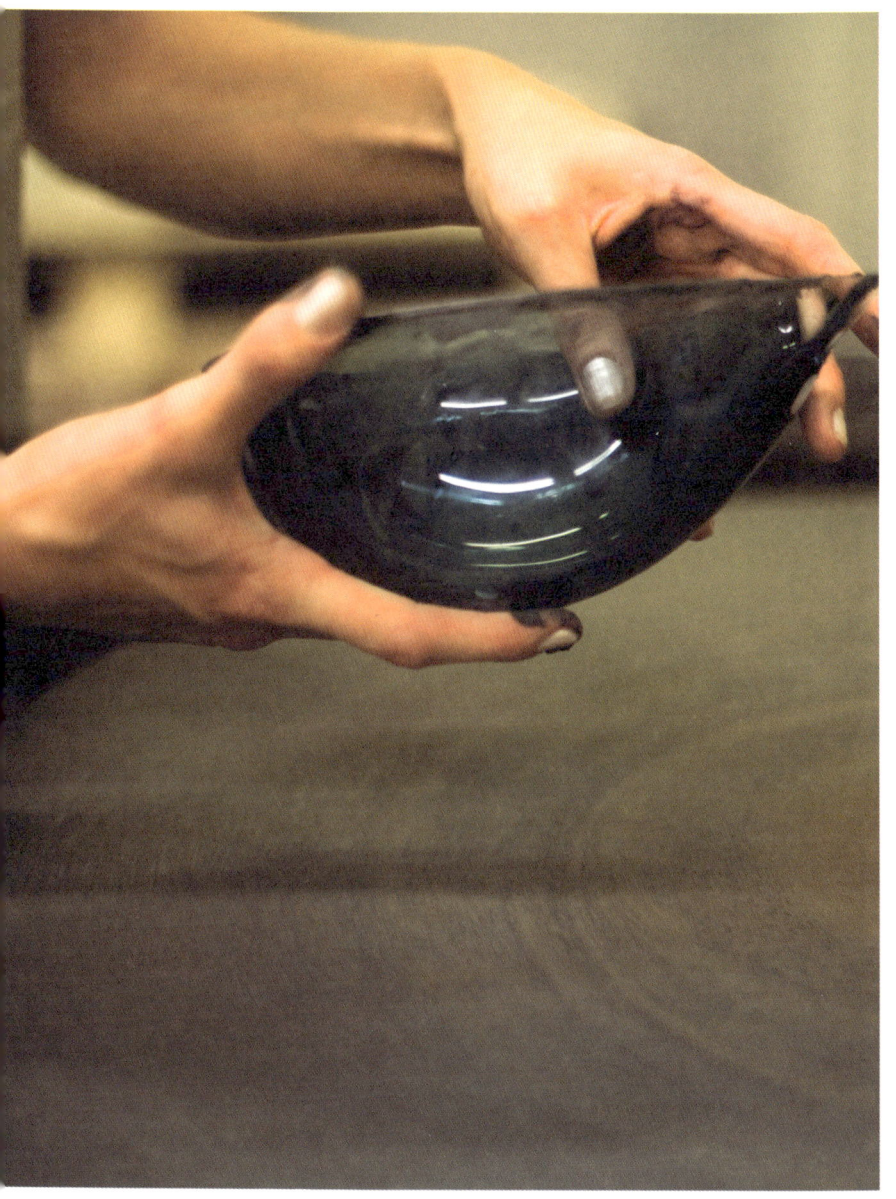

you have to learn about. There's all different types of glass as well. There's lead crystal, soda glasses, window glass. Each different type of glass is incompatible with each other. But, once you've learned what is compatible and you know how to use the glass, then that becomes second nature. You never quite tame it, I suppose, there's always something that can be unexpected —that might go wrong— but I think that's part of the fun of working with it, you never really get bored. It's just a really interesting material, and the results are always quite beautiful as well. It's just something I work with and have done for the last ten years, really. I can't imagine doing anything else.

       I first came across glass when I was studying a degree in three-dimensional design which covered everything from wood, metal, ceramics and product design for industry and glass. I think we came across glass at the end of our first year of study. I went into the hot glass studio and watched a demonstration of the hot glass being made, and just found it absolutely fascinating. I instantly fell in love with the material and I've been working with it ever since. You do tend to have a love-hate relationship with it because it's so hard to use, there are so many different techniques. But it's such a beautiful material, it's quite magical, and I think, once you're into it, you're sort of addicted really.

Keira Rathbone, Typewriter Artist
Poole, Dorset

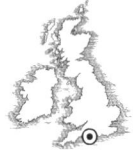

I'm Keira Rathbone and I'm an artist, specialising in typewriter art.

I was studying my fine art degree and I went back home to pick up my typewriter thinking I would use it for writing my sketch book. But, when it came down to it, I didn't have anything to write. So, still really wanting to use my typewriter, I just thought I would see if I could draw with it. That triggered a whole lot of experiments. I started off making portraits out of different characters —brackets and forward slashes, whatever mark suited what I was trying to draw— so, I started using it as a mark-making technique.

The performance element crept in when I decided to take it out of my bedroom and studio, just out and about into the fields, and on the suspension bridge in Bristol, and up the Cabot Tower. I was up there and I just started noticing people's reactions... that it was getting a lot of different reactions from the public. I suddenly decided to develop that. There's a performance element now, definitely. Over the years —because I've been doing it for about six years now— I've started dressing the part as well, sort of in respect to my typewriters. Actually, I've always really liked vintage things, collecting records and such like. So it kind of all fell into place.

I've got about 15 typewriters at the last count. I've got a friend who works at the recycling centre in Wimborne and he phones me when a nice one comes in. He sends me a text with a picture on there and says, "You might wanna come and have a look at this one". It's taking up quite a lot of room at the moment, the idea is that, at my next exhibition, I'm going to have them all in there with the work.

As I was growing up —because I've lived with my mum, and her mum, most of my life— my mum would be typing a letter or

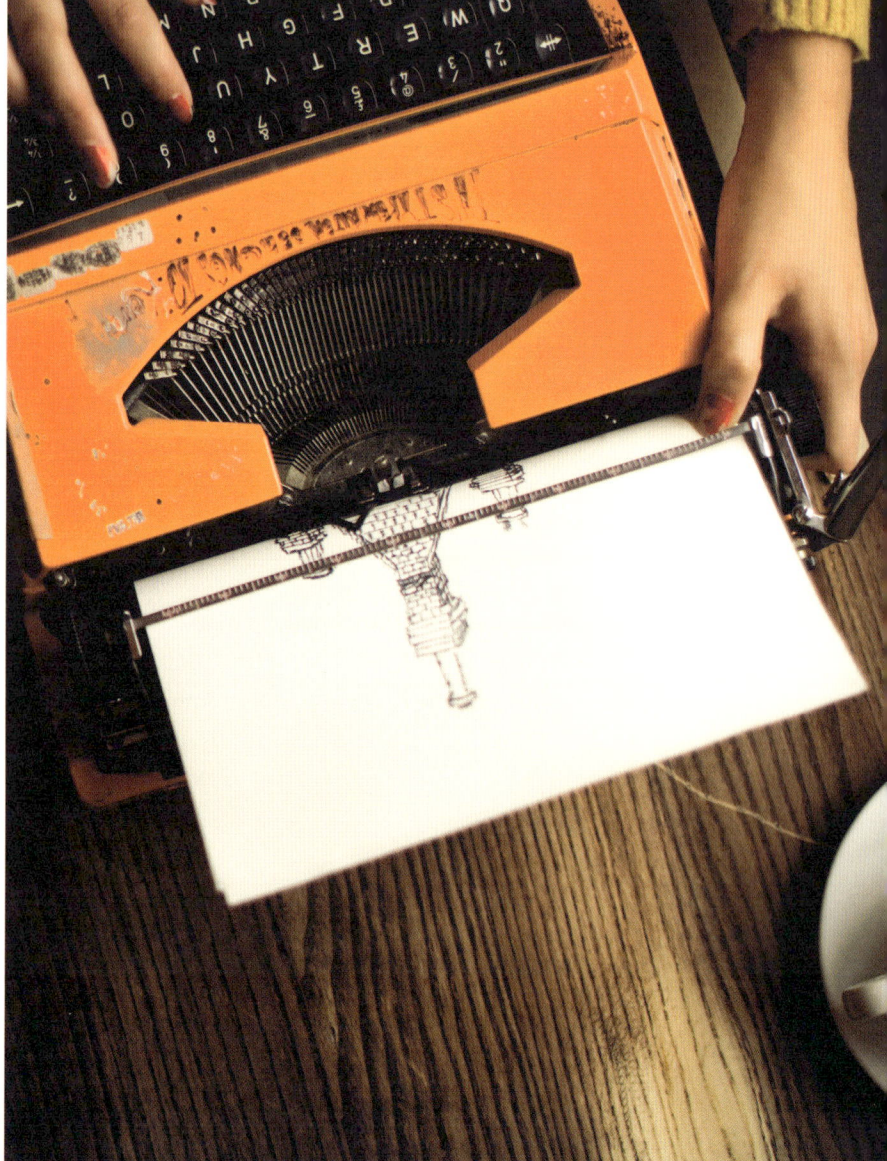

something, or my gran would be writing an airmail letter to someone back in South Africa. So there would always be this tapping —it was really annoying at the time— but typewriters were always there, so I liked playing with them. Never had anything to write though, except maybe "hello". Then there was a massive gap, and then taking up drawing with it just seemed a more natural thing to do with it for me. Although I paint and draw as well, this has become my main art form now. I do love it and I like collecting things, so it's taking over as well. The people I meet when I'm going out and about typing, it's really amazing. All walks of life —children through to elderly people— everyone's got some sort of connection with typewriters.

John J Savage, Storyteller
Holywood, County Down

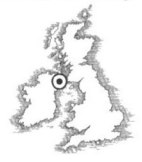

My name is John Johnston Savage. Johnston being my mother's maiden name.

I'm quite proud of John Johnston Savage because I was called after my uncle, who died when he was 22 of leukemia. So I'm named after him. And if I'm signing, I sign John J Savage. That's my full title, I'm known as John. I'm a visitor guide here at Ulster Folk and Transport Museum. I'm here to tell people about the house —and to show people around the house— but I also do storytelling. I'm a traditional storyteller. Fairies, banshees, ghosts... that type of thing, that's my forte as far as storytelling goes, and it's thoroughly enjoyable.

Champ is a very basic food. It's made with, what we call here in Ireland, scallion, but generally in the rest of the UK we call it spring onion. Now, the way I was taught to do champ, you actually cut off the onion bit —you cut off the bulb, you discard the bulb— and use the green stalks. That was the way I was taught to do it. Other people tell me that's wrong, and I will not agree with them. So basically what we have, it would have been a dish that was very easy to make, very cheap and very common. Coming from Ireland, of course we had lots of potatoes. So it's your boiled potatoes, your scallions, chopped up. Now generally, they would soften them in some milk —boil them in milk— and then add that to the potato with some butter, salt, pepper, seasoning and mash it. I didn't have a small pot to soften my scallions in milk, so actually what I did was I sautéed them —I fried them a little bit— in a pan with a little butter, just to soften them. So it's a dish which, I suppose, is now looked upon as a traditional Irish dish along with Irish Stew and Irish Fry or Irish Breakfast. Up here we call it Ulster Fry. It's one thing we're very good at. We're very good at making food that gives us heart attacks.

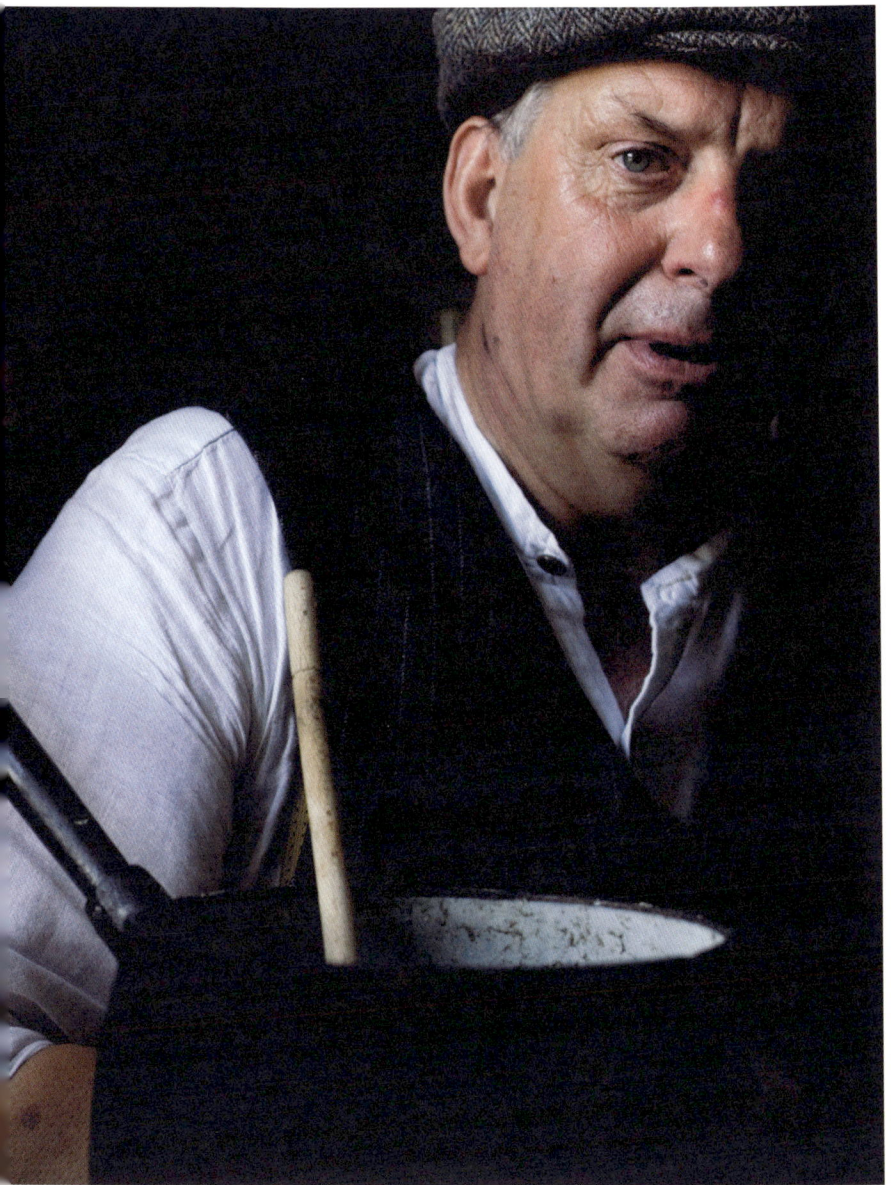

We're very, very fortunate here in the museum. We have got archive material from old storytellers, old Irish storytellers, who have long gone. They've gone to tell their stories somewhere else, in the sky. But we have archives, we have it recorded, and we have it written down. So we can go to our archive and listen to these old boys telling stories and read what they're saying. Now, the stories will differ. The main thrust of the story will be the same but, of course, if I tell you a story, if I tell you about something which happened —or if you told me something that happened on your journey here, and it's important, perhaps— I'll then go and tell that to someone else, but I'll put a different slant on it. Typically, if these older storytellers told stories that related to their living conditions, their townland perhaps, and they'd say, "Oh, the following story happened in Killynether", because that was local to them. When I go to tell that, I will say, "Oh, it happened in Ballyeasborough" —which is a townland closer to me— just to try and give a little bit of local connection. So, the things change a little bit and stories which have maybe six or seven versions, the main thrust's the same. That's the beauty of it because people will then call me and say, "I know that story, but I know it as...", something different. And you can build on that because the next time you tell it, you may tell their version of it. You may swap the two around a little bit.

Without sounding soft or wimpish about it, this is a lovely job. You know, I'm paid to sit and talk to people. My role is to come in, in the morning, light that fire and sit and wait for people to come and talk to me. A couple of years ago, one Saturday, I'd been working away and got home and I was sitting in the garden having a beer and I started counting. I'd spoke to people from 13 different countries in the one afternoon and you don't get that anywhere else. It's meeting people, and everyone has a story to tell you. You know, people often say to me, "How did you become a storyteller?" I don't know how I became storyteller, because everyone has a story to tell. Even children are storytellers. When they tell you something that's happened, they elaborate on it, you know? They make it a bit more flowery. Their imagination runs away. Hopefully, what the museum is trying to do, we're trying to bring back this tradition of people sitting around, having a chat and telling a story. If I tell something, they say, "Oh, that reminds me of something my mother told me…", or something like that and it takes it on.

As far as I'm concerned, I couldn't get a better job, couldn't get a better job in the world, than sitting and talking to people every day. And you never know who's going to come through the door. I'll just say this as well, it's been a pleasure talking to you. It's nice to meet people, and that's just the way I feel about it.

Peter Segger, Organic Farmer
Aberaeron, Ceredigion

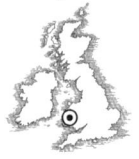

My name's Peter, Peter Segger and with my partner Anne Evans, we have been farming this little bit of wonderful paradise in West Wales —about three miles from the coast of Aberaeron— organically, since 1974.

We were one of the first certified organic farms in Britain and we've been doing it ever since. It's a beautiful place. It's a small farm, it's only 50 acres, we grow about 15 acres of vegetables and we have a large amount of greenhouses. It's a family farm. The children now —as we are getting older— come to work on the farm and work at the farmers' markets. We have a beautiful little place with woodland and streams and a wonderful environment that we nurture, and which absolutely, I'm in love with every day. Especially with this sort of weather. To walk around at this time of year and smell the hedgerows, and the elderflower, and the honeysuckle. It's like a dream. You could never imagine anything so beautiful.

Here, we're down in the compost site and I suppose —I don't suppose, I know— that this is the essence of everything we do, because if we feed the soil, that's the basic difference. I'm a soil freak. All my life is about soil, working with soil. I mean, the basic land we have here is amongst the poorest in Britain. It's grade four agricultural land, but we've made it work. We've grown vegetables, made a living and we're expanding it now. But it's changed a lot, we used to be like most farmers. In the beginning, there was no organic movement. We were here, so we thought —with some other people— we'd get together and we would produce vegetables on a large scale, take them to the supermarkets —because that's where people go to shop— make them available to everybody, in quite a sort of democratic way, if you like. And to do that, we have to grow —on this small area— quite large volumes of very

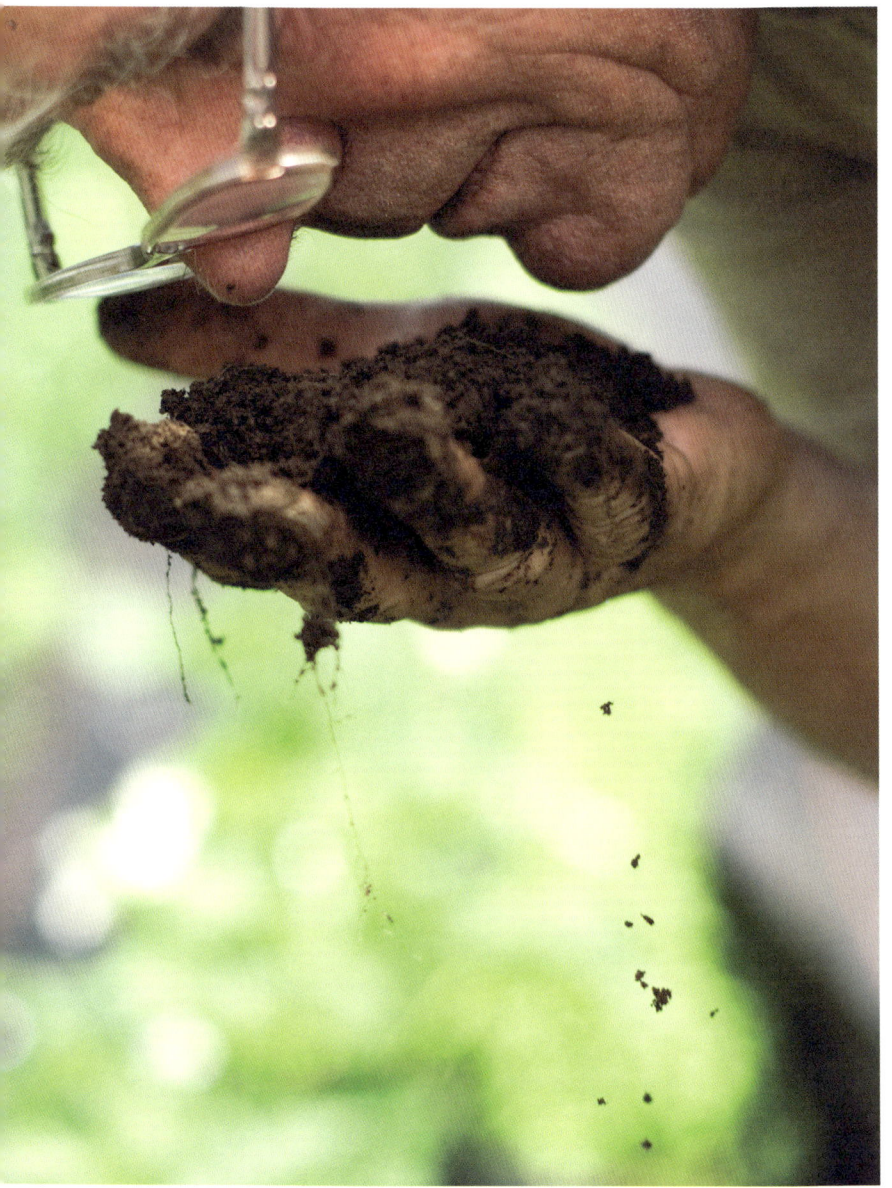

few crops. We would grow greenhouses full of cherry tomatoes in the summertime, and fields of courgettes, and maybe broccoli. Maybe only three or four or five crops in a very large volume. I was also responsible for developing the market, the supermarkets, the wholesale markets and the organic shops through my business in the early eighties. This went on and it expanded and, as we know, organic food — you can find everywhere today.

But there are some things that were always concerning me which were, how do we make our farm resilient in the long term? How do we actually have something that's economically, environmentally and socially sustainable and, in addition, contributing to the culture of the community that we live in? When we looked at ourselves, we actually weren't that sustainable in reality. We were buying in organic chicken manure, we were buying in all our composts, we were buying in lime. I mean, all the things that all farmers do, and organic farmers included. We thought, well it's not really very good. We're also buying in controls —biological controls— to control pests and diseases and I thought, well, if we have an economic problem in the future, can we continue to do that? Then, of course, latterly we got involved in the whole peak oil question and climate change. And then we realised. Yes, we don't use fertilisers —that's oil— but we're still importing a lot.

So we changed. We changed everything. We re-localised all our marketing from everything going to supermarkets or English box schemes to nothing going out of Wales. Opening our own little farm shop —it's an honesty box system where people come along and help themselves— people are wonderful, incredibly honest. We do farmers' markets, the children got involved, they do the farmers' market. So we've re-localised and we will continue to re-localise so that everything from the farm is sold in our community over the next five years.

The basis of doing all that is —what you see in front of you— compost. It's about feeding the soil. We changed some years ago and today we have no inputs at all. We buy in nothing except seed. Nothing. We are one of the few farms in Britain that have almost no inputs. But it rests on this compost. Basically, on your left here, you will see the beginnings of the ingredients of compost. Waste. What people call waste. These are wood chips that come from our hedges in the winter, every seven years we trim the hedges. We don't burn them like most people, we chip them, bring them here. We have grass cuttings from local people and landscape gardeners. They usually take it off and put it in a pile and let it rot, and emit all sorts of greenhouse gasses. We bring it here. We bring grass from the fields, we grow green manures to cut and bring here. We have manures from stables that people don't want, we have cardboard boxes from the local organic shop, we have Christmas trees after Christmas. Any sort of biological waste that we can get, and we convert all that into what you see over there, is black, dark humus.

All we're doing is two basic things. Taking carbon from the atmosphere and putting it into the ground, because there's more carbon in the soil in Britain than there is in the trees, in the atmosphere, or anywhere else. Most carbon —other than sea, oceans— is in the soil, and it's very low. Our priorities are to bring that much out of the atmosphere... to bring that 387 parts per million that exist in air, down to as near to 300 as we can get so that we have a planet for the future. Otherwise we're in trouble. This is the easiest, technologically least complicated thing to do, but it also brings biology into the soil because the humus is just an incredible collection of bacteria and fungi, and the source of all plant food. When you go into that compost, you think it just looks like nice soil, smells alright, but it's just teaming with billions of bacteria, more than there are people on the planet and you're feeding this into the soil to make the soil active. To continue to attract carbon dioxide from the atmosphere, and to feed your plants and, more importantly, to protect them. Because what you want is diversity in nature. For years we've been all about singularity, but it's not about that, it's diversity. Everything you can possibly get, you want every bacteria, every type of fungi, and then each of these has a role in nature, every single one. We only know about the roles of maybe ten per cent. That's enough to tell us. If we've got that ten per cent we'll protect ourselves against most diseases. The pests are controlled by the environment —the hedges, the flowers— all that, and we grow great food. And that's all we do.

Pat Tanner, Boat Builder
Cork City, County Cork

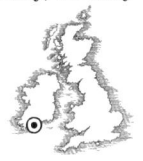

My name is Pat Tanner. I'm a traditional boat builder.

What we've done here is set up a community-based employment scheme, where we have everything from people coming from the social welfare who are out of work, to people that are recovering from substance abuse. Every walk of life, and a place to set up base, as a method of getting people back into the workforce. You've got all different levels of ability, and skill, and interest as well.

What we're hoping to do is to try and keep going the whole tradition and knowledge of wooden boat building. We're repairing and building wooden boats, which are becoming quite an endangered species at the moment. I think there are only two or three boat yards in the country that will repair wooden boats anymore. So, approximately two years ago, Paul contacted me and asked me, would I be willing to come in and teach a bit of wooden boat building? It was supposed to be for two weeks, I'm here two years or more now.

So, we have a group of about six people who've come from different backgrounds, some of them have done a one-year long boat building course in a VEC school, and then want to extend that to learn more of the trade, more woodworking and boat building. Other people have just come with no woodworking experience at all. We start them off with basic woodworking and making a simple item, like a shelf or a stool, and if they're interested and willing to continue, they go on to work with the team in boat building and repairing. Basically, anything from minor repair —sand down and a coat of paint and freshen up the paintwork— all the way up to a complete rebuild of a boat. We have one example, a little twelve-foot rowing boat. 'Twas gone too rotten, 'twas gone beyond repairing, so we thought the best solution would be to measure the boat

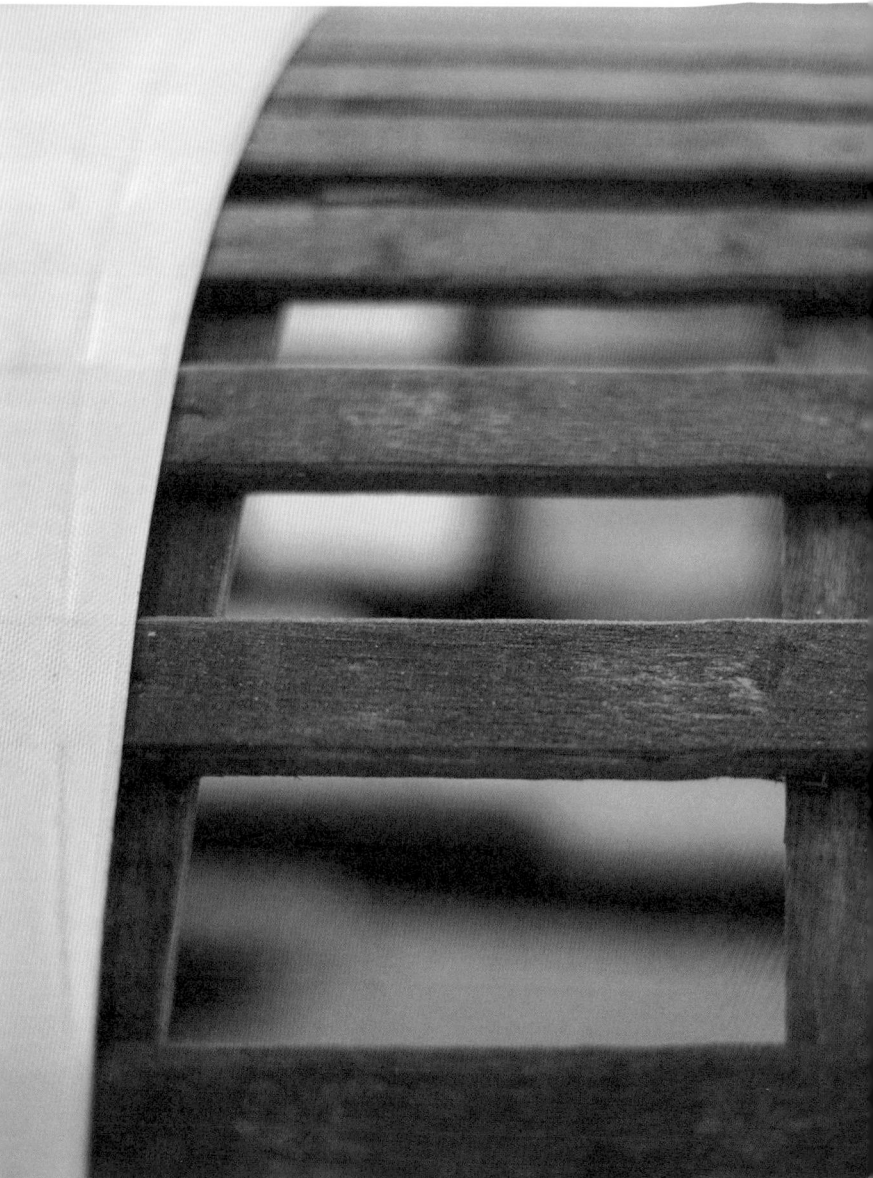

and rebuild it completely from scratch. So, we finished that about six months ago and the owner was quite happy with the end result.

We have a 25-foot sailing yacht, they're known as a folkboat, they're originally built in Norway. There'd still be quite a lot of them around, they're a popular little weekend cruising boat. That boat, it had been neglected for a couple of years, left out in the weather and all the deck area was badly damaged from rainwater. The water had gotten in under the plywood deck and started rotting the deck beams and everything. So we took that on as a job to strip down all the deck, remove and replace all the rotten timber, and rebuild and restore it back to, hopefully, as good as, or better than, its original condition. Basically you're taking a boat that would have been borderline whether she was worth saving. To go to a commercial boat yard and pay commercial rates, the cost of the repair would probably have been greater than the value of the boat and by doing the job here, where we're not charging full commercial rates —because we're using it as a training project as well— so we tell the customers, you still get a properly done, correct job, but it'll be slower, so therefore we'll charge a reduced rate. We use it as a training exercise for the lads to learn. So, as a result of that, we're able to restore and maintain a boat that would have been very borderline whether it was worth saving or not. So hopefully we're helping to keep a lot of boats afloat that mightn't have survived.

The canvas on those rowing corricks may have a lifespan of maybe three or four years before the canvas would start to rot away, so there's two of them in here at the moment. You strip off the old canvas and then, at the same time, if there's any timber work that's damaged or rotten, you replace that and refit a new canvas in its entirety.

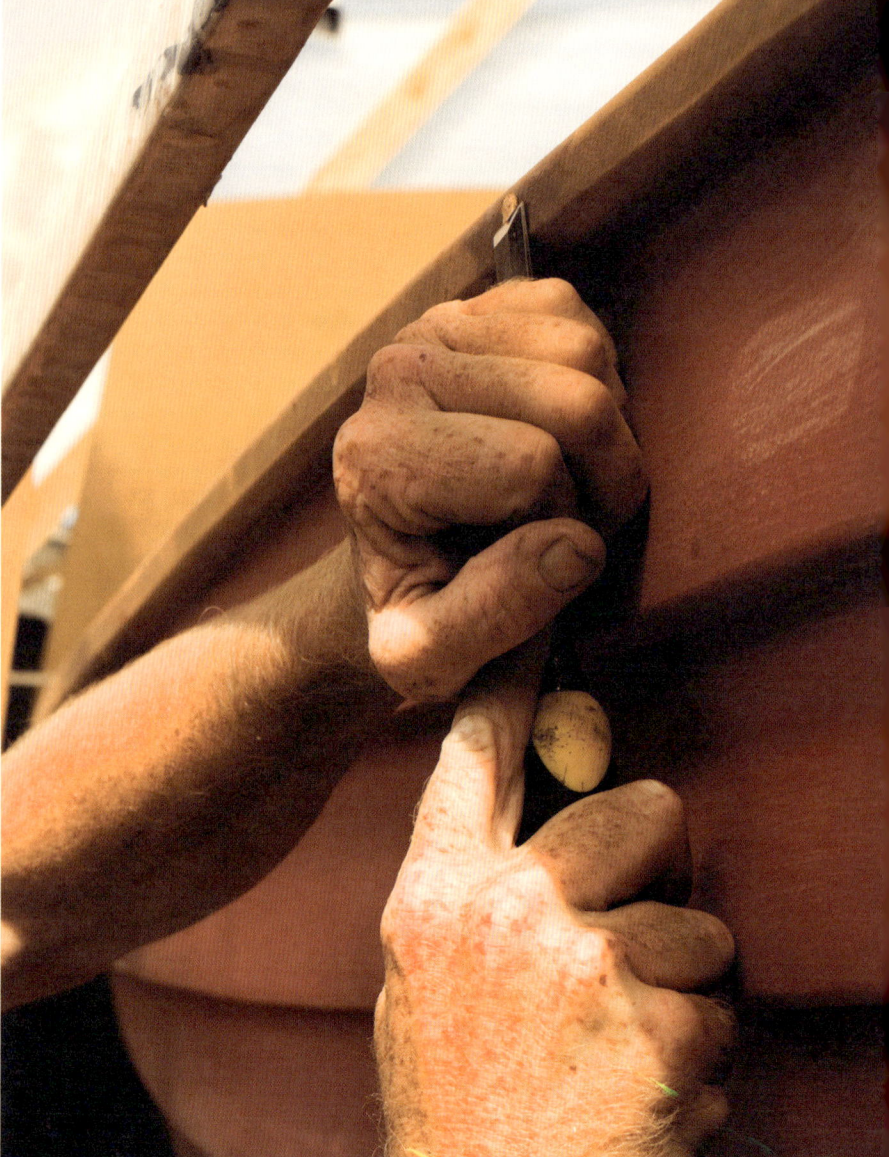

It's gotten to the stage where there's only a handful of boat builders left in the country so there are, quite literally, less than a dozen people who are building traditional wooden boats and a lot of them are reaching retirement age at this stage, so it's nice to be in a place like this, where you have a group of young people who are still interested and willing to learn the skills and trade involved to keep it going. Hopefully there'll be someone there to maintain my boat when I retire.

They are part of our whole maritime heritage — wooden boats have been around a long time before there was any fibreglass or steel boats, and there are some beautiful examples around. They've gone through an awful long period of development where they got refined from the basic canoe, double canoe shape, into purer, elegant racing yachts. There's hundreds of years of refining and developing and improving. It'll be an awful shame to see all that disappear and be replaced with mass-produced plastic boats coming out of factories in Taiwan and China. So there's a skill there and a lot of work and expertise going into building them. You take something like a tree from a forest, and you chop it down, and shape it into a beautiful sailing boat. It'll be a shame and a disgrace for all that to be lost and given up for the sake of cheap, mass-produced... I won't quite call them rubbish, but they're not far off. That's my opinion.

Pip Weaser, Basket Maker
Kilmelford, Argyll and Bute

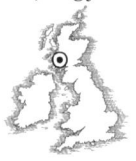

My name is Pip Weaser and I make baskets.

This is a Shetland Kishie, made on Shetland where there's hardly any wood, so they've had to make baskets by using bundles of oat straw tied together with this stuff. It's lovely, got a lovely name. It's called Flossie Simmons, the Simmons is the string and the Flossie is the type of rush, just that rush that's growing out there. So I make a lot of string from different plants in the garden. And the colours are the actual colours of the plant, there's no paint or anything. That's a technique of making string, but linking it together in a shape as you go.

It's about the whole place and the time of year, and about me. I'm actually quite interested in the relationship between place, plants and the people. With the Kishie you make it to fit your own size, the bundles are the size of your hands and when you make this string —the Flossie Simmons— you have to make 22 metres of it. The man who told me about it said it was 22 fathoms. So I said, "What's a fathom?" And he held his arms apart and said, "This is a fathom!" So, it automatically ends up fitting the person who made it.

As far as I'm concerned nothing is taboo. I can put anything in a basket. I like making a basket of stuff that's grown, or recycled, like that paper — that's the Oban Times made into a basket. Everything in the garden can get used. This time of year it's stuff like this, the iris leaves that would be harvested. Most of that's mine, some of it is from Barfad Willow at Ardfern, and when I go in their barn I see it all stacked up in lovely colours, I just want to take it.

I'm very interested in the scientific names of them all when I'm looking at a catalogue or in an official collection, but I hate labels everywhere in the garden, so I forget. Tend to just call it by the

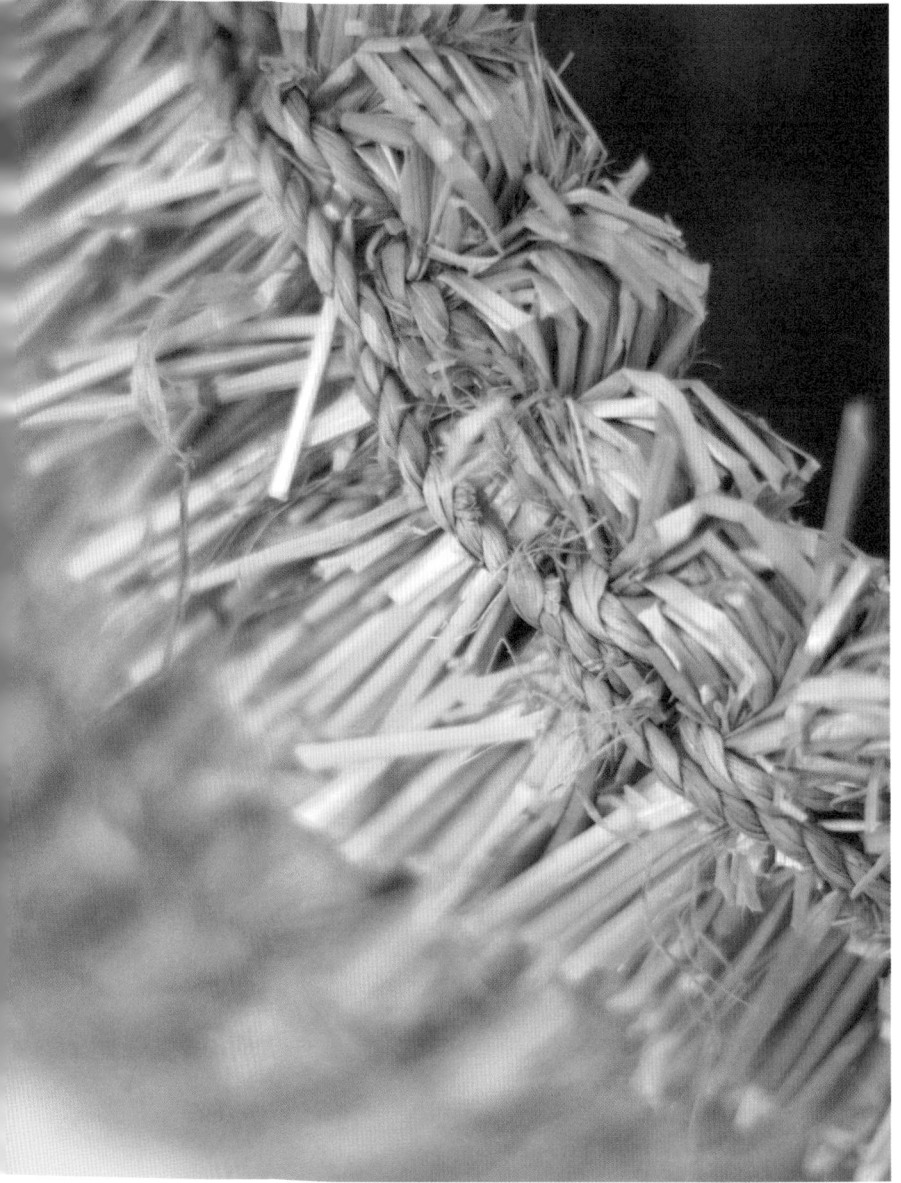

person who gave it to me. So that's Trevor's willow, I might have Maddy's Willow and so on.

There are people who had been forced to make things from the plants that were around them since the year dot. They put grass on the floor to keep it a bit warmer, then they wove it into mats, and they had to make clothes, things to carry stuff, to store food. That has just been passed down from generation to generation. It's getting very, very weak now and I'd quite like to be part of helping pass that on. I wouldn't say that I'm at all skilled. I've got huge respect for traditional basket makers who could sit all day —12 hours a day— and turn out eight log baskets. I definitely don't do that, but I think I can appreciate what they do, and I know some techniques, and I know more techniques than a lot of other people, so I'm able to pass it on a little bit. What I really like is passing it on and seeing somebody get very enthusiastic and taking it further. I find that very rewarding. In fact, I often say I make basket makers, not baskets. It's just absolutely wonderful to see somebody learning to make stuff with their hands, whether they're three years old or 80. There's a lot of people now who never ever make anything and they're just overcome with the fact that they can. They think that there's some huge, innate skill you need when actually, there's a little bit of common sense, and a bit of practice, and a bit of help. And to know that they can make stuff from their prunings in the gardens is great fun.

I love the whole cycle of growing stuff —harvesting and making it— so a lot of my work isn't at all functional, it's just that I love the colour, and feel, and smell of the plant, or the lichen, depending on the time of year. I love the colour and I just want to make it into something that will capture that.

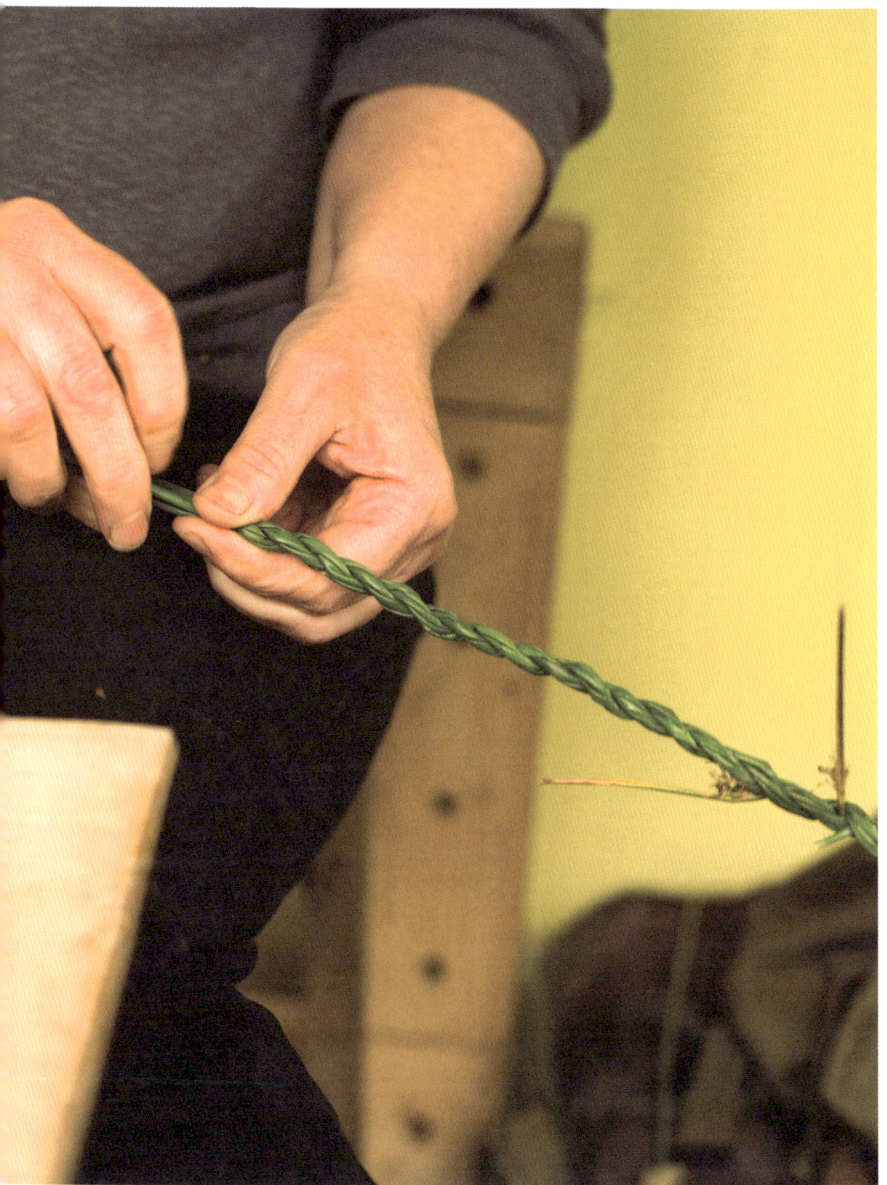

The full series

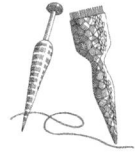

The original photofilms of the artists and craftspeople in this book are available to view at www.slowcoast.co.uk. Here, the full series is listed in the order that they were made — starting from Bristol, and travelling clockwise around the coast.

England

Merlin Crossingham
Creative Director
Aardman Animations
Bristol

Wales

**Marcus Beck and
Simon Macro**
Designers
Freshwest Design
Tenby, Pembrokeshire

Clare Hieatt
Director
Howies
Cardigan, Ceredigion

Peter Segger
Organic Farmer
Blaencamel Farm
Aberaeron, Ceredigion

John Parry
Volunteer
Dyfi Osprey Project
Machynlleth, Powys

Chris Morton
Centre for Alternative
Technology
Machynlleth, Powys

Allan Moller
Musician and Reed Maker
Uilleann Reeds
Blaenau Ffestiniog,
Gwynedd

Bea Williams
Soap Maker
You're Gorgeous
Glan Conwy, Conwy

England

**Visitors to Anthony
Gormley's *Another Place***
Crosby, Merseyside

**Visitors to Eric
Morecambe's memorial**
Morecambe, Lancashire

Harold Cunningham
Red Squirrel Feeder
Workington, Cumbria

Alan Walker
Rabbit Catcher
Kirkbride, Cumbria

Scotland

Graham King
Around Britain Kayaker
Kirkudbright,
Dumfries and Galloway

Joanna and Donald Gisbey
Artist and Musician
Auchencairn,
Dumfries and Galloway

**Stephanie Diver
and Midge McKeachie**
Cyclists
Border City Wheelers
Portpatrick,
Dumfries and Galloway

Ronnie Bowie
Bike Shop Owner
Stranraer,
Dumfries and Galloway

John McKenna
Sculptor
Turnberry, Ayrshire

Hans
Cyclist
Lochranza, Isle of Arran

James MacTaggart
Master Distiller
Isle of Arran Distillers
Isle of Arran

Alan McDougall
Smoker
The Old Smokehouse
Campbeltown,
Argyll and Bute

Jo McLean
Programme Producer
Cove Park
Cove, Argyll and Bute

Sheena Devitt
Stone Letter Carver
Lochgilphead,
Argyll and Bute

Louise Oppenheimer
Weaver
Kilmartin, Argyll and Bute

Mary McAlister Hall
Tanner
Torrisdale Tannery
Carradale,
Argyll and Bute

Pip Weaser
Basket Maker
Kilmelford, Argyll and Bute

John MacPherson
Weaver
Lochcarron Weavers
Lochcarron, Highlands

Paul from Chesterfield
Cyclist
Scourie, Highlands

Julian Pearce
Shorehouse Restaurant
Tarbet, Highlands

Lotte Glob
Ceramic Artist
Laid, Highlands

Jenna Hume
Knitted Textile Designer
Hume Sweet Hume
Westray, Orkney

Fraser Anderson
Strawback Chair Maker
Orkney Hand Crafted
Furniture
Kirkwall, Orkney

Jackie Miller
Strawback Chair Maker
Scapa Crafts
Kirkwall, Orkney

Joanne B Kaar
Paper Maker and Artist
Dunnet, Highlands

Sue Jane Taylor
Visual Artist
Achavandra, Highlands

Tilda Swinton
and Mark Cousins
A Pilgrimage
Nairn, Highlands

Avalon dos Santos
Findhorn Foundation
Findhorn, Moray

Bill Spink
Fish Merchant
M&M Spink
Arbroath, Angus

Kay Anderson
Spinner
Arbroath, Angus

James Yorkston
and Kenny Anderson
The Fence Collective
Fife

Douglas Grierson
Master Weaver
Dovecot Studios
Edinburgh

Howie R Nicholsby
Kilt Designer
21st Century Kilts
Edinburgh

England

Joanne Mitchell
Glass Maker
Sunderland

Chris and Neil Cobbett
Coast to Coast Riders
Sunderland

Keith Hannah
Trailways Cycle Hire
and Sales
Whitby, North Yorkshire

David Cooper
Master Blacksmith
DC Blacksmiths
Bridlington, East Yorkshire

Bill Bontoft
Stickmaker
Manby, Lincolnshire

Mr Aylesbury
Auction on the Green
Burnham Market, Norfolk

David Hewitt
Boat Builder
Stiffkey, Norfolk

Paul Smith
Designer
London

Will Brown
Outfitter
Old Town
Holt, Norfolk

David Morris
Photographer
Cromer, Norfolk

Gunhild Espelage,
Christiane Guenther,
Quay Proctor-Mears,
Rosalind Redfern,
Nicole Schumacher
Ceramicists and Goldsmith
Made in Cley
Cley-next-the-Sea, Norfolk

Cally
Cycle Collector
Walpole, Suffolk

Brian Alabaster
Sculptor
Linstead, Suffolk

Laurence Edwards
Sculptor
Butley, Suffolk

Sarah Green
Organic Farmer
Tillingham, Essex

Suki Hays-Watkins
Printmaker
The Print Block
Whitstable, Kent

Dawn and Erin Hackutt
The Cheese Box
Whitstable, Kent

Zoe Murphy
Hand Printed Furniture
and Textile Designer
Margate, Kent

Martina Gavan
Stained Glass Designer
Hastings, East Sussex

Paul Topham
Specialbike
Hove, West Sussex

Ruth and Annette
Cyclists
Southsea Breakfast Club
Southsea, Hampshire

Keira Rathbone
Typewriter Artist
Poole, Dorset

Billy Bragg
Singer Songwriter
Bridport, Devon

Hugh Dunford Wood
Artist Designer
Lyme Regis, Dorset

Hilary Burns
Basket Maker and Weaver
Paignton, Devon

Jeremy Barker
Ecologist
Slapton Bird Ringing Group
Slapton, Devon

Mervyn Bennallack
Michaelmas Daisy Grower
Tavistock, Devon

Keith Harrison
Ceramicist and
Performance Artist
Plymouth, Devon

Nicola Bradley
Supervisor
The Lost Gardens of Heligan
Pentewan, Cornwall

Louis Hunkin
Boat Builder
WC Hunkin & Sons
Fowey, Cornwall

Mark Roberts
Wooden Surfboard Maker
Glass Tiger Surfboards
Falmouth, Cornwall

Nigel Legge
Fisherman, Artist and
Lobster Pot Maker
Cadgwith Cove, Cornwall

Claire Francis
Hat Maker
Salt Cellar Hats
Porthleven, Cornwall

Fiona Kelly
Dressmaker
Feeline Clothing
Salt Cellar Workshops
Porthleven, Cornwall

Elsie Pinniger
Wetsuit and Clothing
Designer
Neon Wetsuits
Newquay, Cornwall

Sam Lindo
Wine Maker
Camel Valley
Nanstallon, Cornwall

Neil and Gill Faiers
Organic Farmers and
B&B owners
Bangors Organic Bed,
Breakfast and Restaurant
Poundstock, Cornwall

Billy Hawkins
Potter
Port Isaac Pottery
Port Issac, Cornwall

Mikey Corker
Manager
Loose-fit
Braunton, Devon

John Halls
Tea Taster
Miles Tea and Coffee
Merchants
Minehead, Somerset

Northern Ireland

Austin Brown
Bicycle Mechanic
Belfast Bicycle Workshop
Belfast

Martin Carter
Artist in Found Objects
Lawrence Street Workshops
Belfast

**Jackson Conn, Merle
Osbourne and Diane Shaw**
Blacksmith, Spinner
and Weaver
The Ulster Folk and
Transport Museum
Holywood, County Down

John J Savage
Storyteller
The Ulster Folk and
Transport Museum
Holywood, County Down

Karl Harron
Glass Artist
The Glass Studio
Loughries, County Down

Clive Lyttle
Basket Maker and
Countryside Skills
Practitioner
Welig Crafts
Portaferry, County Down

Mike Miall
Windsor Chair Maker
Portaferry, County Down

Darren Cunningham
Oyster Farmer
Carlingford Lough,
County Down

Karen Hay-Edie
Weaver
Mourne Textiles
Newry, County Down

Republic of Ireland

Luke Van Doorslaer
Sonairte, The National
Ecology Centre
Laytown, County Meath

Darren Matthews
Chef
Bon Appétit
Malahide, Dublin

Fearghal O'Nuallain
Round the World Cyclist
Greystones,
County Wicklow

Rory O'Connell
Chef and Teacher
Ballymaloe Cookery School
Shanagarry, County Cork

Pat Tanner
Boat Builder
Meitheal Mara
Cork

Pádraig Ó Duinnín
(Gaelic version)
Boat Builder
Meitheal Mara
Cork

Tom Ferguson
Cheese Maker
Gubbeen Cheese
Schull Market, County Cork

Matt Padwick
Manager
Dzogchen Beara Tibetan
Buddhist Retreat Centre
Allihies, County Cork

Paul F Kelly
Gold and Silversmith
Kenmare, County Kerry

Helen Moriarty
Teddy O'Sullivan's
Kilmackillogue Pier,
County Kerry

Angela and Carl Daly
Kenmare Bay Seafoods
Kilmackillogue Harbour,
County Kerry

Dominique Lieb
Letterpress Printer
Púca Press
Dingle, County Kerry

Chiara Shokite
Fixed Wheel Tourer
Dingle, County Kerry

Martin Doyle
Flute Maker
Martin Doyle Flutes
Liscannor, County Clare

Graham Roberts
Smoker
Connemara Smokehouse
Ballyconneely,
County Galway

Brian O'Grady
Skipper
The Clew Bay Queen
The Clare Island Ferry
Company
Clare Island, County Mayo

Beth Moran
Weaver
Ballytoughey Loom
Clare Island, County Mayo

John Hogan
Artist Blacksmith
Killala, County Mayo

John Joseph Hanna
Hat Maker
Hanna Hats
Donegal Town,
County Donegal

Ailbhe Dunne,
Aideen Fitzpatrick,
Ruth McCartney
Carbon Footprint Project
Carndonagh,
County Donegal

Northern Ireland

John Wilkinson
Canoe Builder
Valkyrie Craft
Coleraine, Londonderry

The Slowcoast series of photofilms
are available to view online
www.slowcoast.co.uk

Further photofilms and
projects by Nick Hand
www.departmentofsmallworks.co.uk

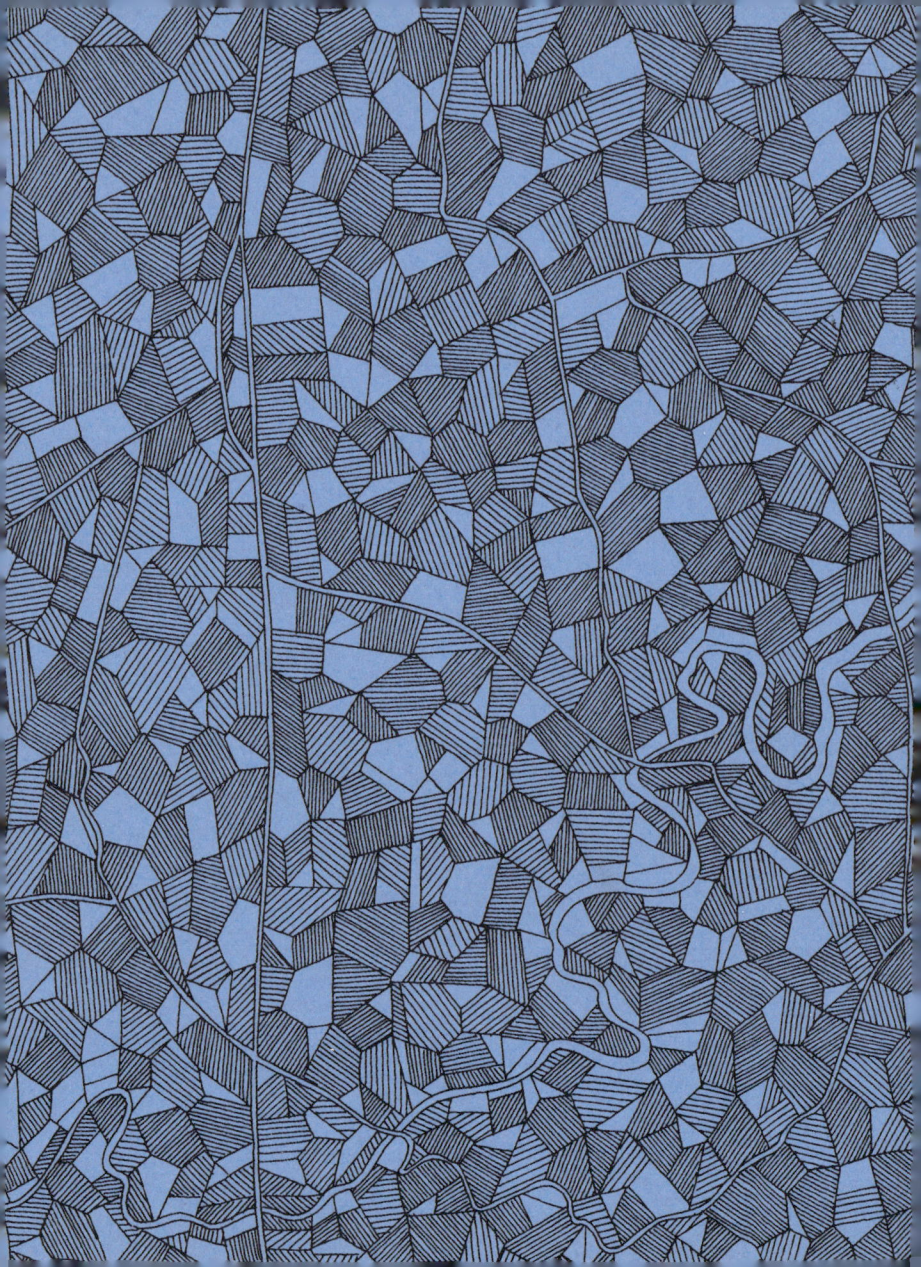